GIVING·GOOD·FOOD

GIVING·GOOD·FOOD

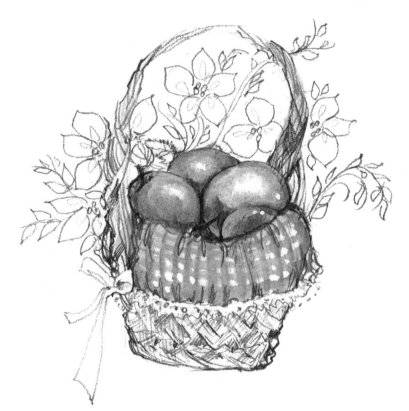

by Deborah Navas

Illustrations by Margo Letourneau

YANKEE BOOKS

a division of Yankee Publishing Incorporated, Dublin, New Hampshire

Designed by Alison Scott
Illustrated by Margo Letourneau

First Edition
Copyright 1984, by Yankee Publishing Incorporated
Printed in the United States of America

Library of Congress Catalog Card Number: 84-50425
ISBN: 0-89909-036-2

With gratitude to my whole family, and especially to Judy.

✖ *TABLE OF CONTENTS* ✖

✄ *INTRODUCTION* ✄

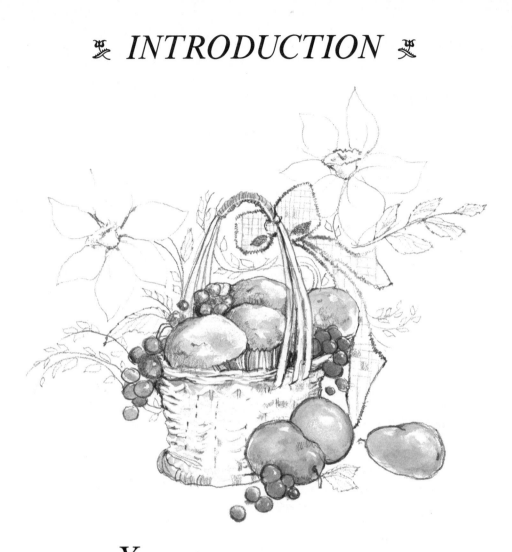

*Y*ears ago, before we became trapped by a standard of living which seems to require expensive store-bought gifts for birthdays, Christmas, and other occasions, gifts were made at home. Gifts for all occasions were constructed, knitted, sewn, cut, and pasted together with loving attention. The kitchen especially was a year-round gift shop.

My own favorite kitchen gift which has lasted, if not a lifetime, then at least twenty years and is still going strong, is a simple recipe box. It was given me by my sister Judy, who threw what she called a "recipe shower" prior to my wedding. She had collected favorite recipes from relatives and family friends by mailing each of them several blank 3x5-inch file cards along with a self-addressed return envelope. Then she gathered the cards that were returned with recipes together in a recipe box, which she wrapped and presented to me.

As a young bride whose cooking skills hovered at zero, I was nonplussed by the gift, but have since come to consider it as one of my most treasured possessions. Every well-worn card, food-spattered and yellowed by time, written in the hand of someone dear to me, evokes a vivid memory of the writer — be it my mother, or grandmother, or mother-in-law, or an old friend. Handwriting is so personal — each card represents a small intimate connection with those I've loved, renewed every time I use the recipe box; all because of a thoughtful and inexpensive gift.

Gifts from the kitchen are a tradition in my family, almost all of whom are talented cooks — from my father, whose fabulous Castilian Seafood Chowder recipe was known only to him until I teased it out of him, to my sister Judy, whose recipe file is two feet long, to my sister-in-law Barbara, whose figures (made from a pre-dyed baker's clay she invented) constitute a thriving small business.

Here are their favorite recipes for gifts from the kitchen — some time-hallowed, some as new as yesterday — along with suggestions regarding particularly suitable occasions and tips on transporting and packaging. Gifts of food are relatively inexpensive, easy to make (meaning I can do them), and best of all, they embody the fine old tradition of giving something of yourself with each gift.

NOTE: Ingredients in italics are those to accompany the gift, to be added at the time the food is served.

Debrah Navas

⚞ *CHAPTER 1* ⚟

Nourishing Gifts — Soups, Chowders, and Casseroles

*N*ourishing foods are appropriate for almost any occasion, a wonderfully practical and much appreciated expression of care and concern. Comfort a sick friend with rich, homemade chicken soup. Ease the burden of bereavement with a hot meal personally delivered. Fill an icebox with ready-cooked fare for friends returning from their travels, bringing home a new baby, or in the throes of moving out or in. Times like these, the appearance of a hearty, easy-to-heat meal can seem like manna from heaven. Combined with a loaf of homemade bread, muffins, or rolls (see Chapter 2), any of the soups, chowders, or casseroles below will provide a delicious meal for at least four adults. See Note at end of Introduction regarding ingredients printed in italics.*

PACKAGING SOUPS, CHOWDERS, AND CASSEROLES

Generally, when my family and I bestow soups, stews, or casseroles as gifts, we deliver them in the pot they were cooked in and retrieve the pot at some later date. This is fine for near neighbors, but for others — better to use foil pans or plastic containers (see below). Whenever you do leave your own dish with the recipient, make sure to state that the dish is to be returned *empty.* This is why — once, somewhere in the dark annals of housewifery, it was ordained that no dish should *ever* be returned empty, so that a gift of food became a not-so-subtle demand for food in return. Therefore make it clear at the outset that you don't subscribe to such perverse theories.

When people live too far afield to return a dish conveniently, often either they'll forget to do so, or you'll forget to retrieve it. Or, perish the thought, perhaps they thought your dearest dutch oven was part of the gift — how do you get around *that*? Far better to find a container that need not be returned. Kitchen specialty shops now carry quite inexpensive 4- and 6-quart jars perfect for soups and chowders, as well as anything — like Curried Chicken — that looks pretty through clear glass. Some things, like Pork Karoki, do not. For those, use the plastic storage containers or disposable foil pans and dishes you can buy in assorted sizes, at supermarkets.

Gifts of food — like any other gift — should be attractively packaged with an appropriate card and message. Because a meal is an eminently practical, basic sort of gift, extraneous decoration like metallic bows on the stockpot lid are not really necessary. Drop off the gift without ceremony; the card enclosed bearing the appropriate sentiment and directions for use will say it all.

Foods in this chapter are not suitable for mailing; mailed gifts will be taken up in following chapters.

SOUPS AND CHOWDERS

⚜ BROCCOLI-CHEESE SOUP ⚜

A hearty soup tailor-made for bringing along to a card party or informal supper with friends. Accompanying instructions should advise not to boil when reheating. Include a sandwich bag of parsley for garnish. Do not freeze.

1 small onion, chopped
1 clove garlic, pressed
4 scallions including 1-2 inches green stem, chopped
1 pound fresh broccoli, florets and tender stems, chopped
¼ pound mushrooms, chopped
4 tablespoons butter
1 tablespoon cooking oil

3 tablespoons flour
2 cups chicken broth
1½ cups milk
½ teaspoon salt
2 cups shredded sharp Cheddar cheese

• • •

several sprigs fresh parsley

In heavy soup pot, sauté onions, garlic, scallions, broccoli, and mushrooms in butter and oil. Sauté, stirring for 5-8 minutes, or until broccoli is tender. Stir in flour and whisk until smooth and bubbly. Gradually whisk in broth, then add milk and salt. Cook until mixture thickens. Add cheese and stir until melted. Heat to steaming, not boiling. Serves 4.

❧ COLD CANTALOUPE SOUP ❧

A mellow fruit soup to refresh a sick friend on a hot day. Include fresh mint in a sandwich bag for garnish. Accompanying instructions should advise to serve cold, in chilled bowls or glasses. Do not freeze.

1 ripe cantaloupe, peeled,
  seeded, and cubed
1 quart apricot juice
juice of 1 lemon
1 tablespoon sugar
¼ teaspoon ginger

¼ teaspoon cinnamon
dash ground cloves
1 cup sour cream
• • •
fresh mint sprigs

In soup pot, place cantaloupe, apricot juice, lemon juice, sugar, ginger, cinnamon, and cloves. Cover pot and simmer 30 minutes. Puree mixture in blender and cool. Beat in sour cream and chill thoroughly. Serves 6-8.

❧ SUPER RICH CORN CHOWDER ❧

Better, or leastways richer than mother used to make. Not to be given to those who worry about cholesterol levels, nor to dieters. Don't forget to include the salt pork garnish in a sandwich bag. Accompanying instructions: reheat by a gentle simmer — no rolling boil.

¼ pound salt pork, cut in ¼-
  inch cubes
2 medium onions, chopped fine
2 medium potatoes, peeled and
  cut into ½-inch dice
10-ounce package frozen corn
17-ounce can creamed corn
1 cup beef stock

2 cups half & half
1 cup milk
⅓ cup sour cream
1 teaspoon sugar
salt and pepper
• • •
fried salt pork for garnish

In 6-quart kettle, fry salt pork cubes until brown; take pork out with slotted spoon, drain on paper towel, and save for garnish. Sauté onions in pork fat, then add potatoes, frozen and canned corn, and beef stock. Cover and simmer 15 minutes. Add cream, milk, sour cream, sugar, and salt and pepper to taste. Heat just to boiling point. Serves 4.

✵ MADELINE'S ITALIAN CHICKEN SOUP ✵

Enriched with meatballs and noodles, this is the best chicken soup I have ever tasted — the perfect gift for nursing mothers or ailing friends. Freeze and reheat with abandon. An accompanying jar of hand-grated Parmesan cheese to sprinkle over the soup just before serving is a nice added touch.

SOUP

2½- to 3-pound chicken
1 quart water
4 stalks of celery with tops
3 or 4 carrots, sliced
1 large onion, chopped
1 clove garlic
1 bay leaf
½ teaspoon thyme

3 eggs
¾ pound greens: escarole, chicory, or spinach
1½ cups thin egg noodles
salt and pepper

• • •

Parmesan cheese

MEATBALLS

¼ pound lean hamburger
¼ pound ground pork
1 egg
½ cup Italian-seasoned bread crumbs

1 teaspoon chopped fresh parsley
½ teaspoon salt
¼ teaspoon ground pepper
½ teaspoon oregano
¼ teaspoon basil

Cut chicken in quarters and wash. Cook in quart of water, with celery, carrots, onion, garlic, bay leaf, thyme, and 3 eggs (in their shells) for 25 minutes, or until meat is tender. While the chicken is cooking, combine meatball ingredients. Form meat mixture into tiny balls about ¾ inch round. Brown in a lightly oiled frying pan.

When chicken is tender remove it from pot, and discard bay leaf and half the celery. Cool, skin, and bone chicken and cut meat into small pieces. Take one of the hardboiled eggs from the broth, chop up, and return to pot. Take the other two hardboiled eggs from the broth and set aside. Run chicken broth, chopped egg, carrots, etc. through a blender, and return blended broth to the pot. Add cut-up chicken, browned meatballs, greens, and egg noodles; bring to boil, cover, and cook 5-8 minutes, or until greens and noodles are done, stirring often to prevent sticking. Shell and slice remaining two hardboiled eggs and add to broth. Season to taste with salt and pepper. Serves 6-8.

☙ CONSOMMÉ AUX TOMATES ☙

An elegant soup deceptively easy to make. The acidic tomato base is good for colds and flu, and the sherry doesn't hurt either. My sister Judy thought up this one. If you want to be really fancy, include some curls of lemon rind in a plastic bag for garnish.

16-ounce can tomatoes
½ cup unsalted sherry
1 medium onion, sliced
1 clove garlic, pressed
1 stalk celery, chopped
1 carrot, sliced
1 tablespoon butter
½ teaspoon sugar

½ teaspoon salt
1 bay leaf
3 whole cloves
2 cups beef stock*
½ cup orange juice
1 cup tomato juice
• • •
lemon rind

In heavy 2-quart saucepan, put tomatoes, sherry, onion, garlic, celery, carrot, butter, sugar, salt, bay leaf, and cloves. Cover and simmer 35 minutes. Discard bay leaf and cloves, and whirl soup in blender. Add remaining ingredients and simmer 30 minutes. Serves 6.

* If you use canned beef broth or bouillon, be sure to dilute if the instructions on the can so specify.

☙ KALE SOUP ☙

A good friend, Anne LeClaire, gave me this recipe when she heard it was my husband's favorite. This is a full-flavored hearty soup, not recommended for those with a delicate palate. It may be frozen, and actually improves with age.

½ pound dry kidney beans
water to cover
4 cups beef stock
2 bunches or bags of fresh kale, chopped
½ pound chourico, cut into ¼-inch slices

½ pound linguiça, cut into ¼-inch slices
2 medium potatoes, peeled and diced
2 tablespoons cider vinegar
salt and pepper

Soak kidney beans overnight in water to cover. Next morning, drain off water. In large, covered soup pot, simmer beans in beef broth 1 hour. Add kale and sausages, cover, and simmer 2 hours more. Then add remaining ingredients, and simmer 1 hour longer. If liquid cooks down too much, add water. Serves 4-6.

✕ *FISH CHOWDER* ✕

Around New England, chowder recipes are as personal as fingerprints; only to an outlander do they all seem alike. Instructions acompanying this chowder should caution against boiling when reheating, because the fish would become mushy. Include the salt pork garnish in a sandwich bag.

1 pound white fish (pollock, haddock, or whatever's on sale)
¾ cup water
¼ pound salt pork, diced
1 large onion, chopped
2 medium potatoes, peeled and cut in ½-inch dice
1 bay leaf

pinch of thyme
1 teaspoon salt
pepper
1 cup milk
1 cup evaporated milk
2 shakes Angostura bitters

• • •

fried salt pork for garnish

Steam or boil fish in water 5-8 minutes, or until done (don't overcook). Reserve water; remove and bone fish. In a soup kettle, sauté salt pork until golden; set aside. Sauté onion in pork fat, then pour off half the fat. Add potatoes, bay leaf, thyme, salt, and pepper to onion, along with ½ cup of the reserved fish water. Cover and cook 10 minutes, or until potatoes are tender. Then add boned fish, milk, and bitters; heat just to boiling. Discard bay leaf. Serves 6.

⚘ SIDNE'S SUMMER GARDEN SOUP ⚘

Sidne Lewis, my friend and business partner, served me this soup for lunch one day, and it was memorable. Every ingredient except the wine was home-grown by Sidne — from the chicken she raised and slaughtered herself, to the vegetables and herbs from her lavish garden. You don't have to have a home-grown chicken, but you do need fresh herbs and vegetables. This soup may be frozen, but it is really best when served fresh.

1 chicken, cut in pieces	12 Japanese radishes
3 cups dry white wine	1 tablespoon chopped fresh
1 cup water	summer savory
1 bunch Swiss chard	2 teaspoons chopped fresh
½ pound green peas	oregano

In covered stock pot, simmer chicken in wine and water for an hour. (You can use the chicken back and neck to make stock to reserve for other purposes; simmer back and neck in liquid to cover, using the same 3 to 1 — wine to water — proportions.) When the chicken is cooked, bone and skin it, reserving meat for other use. Skim remaining broth, and add vegetables and herbs. Bring just to boil, reduce heat, cover, and simmer 15 minutes more. This soup can accommodate about any vegetable in the garden, but Sidne advises against using more than two herbs at a time, lest they mask each other's flavors. Serves 4.

⚘ GAZPACHO ⚘

An easy recipe for the classic Spanish chilled soup. You may freeze this soup, but it will need a quick trip through your blender to bring back its original creamy state. Your note to the recipient should advise that this soup may be served either hot or chilled.

1-pound can tomatoes with juice	1 cup chopped celery
10½-ounce can consommé	2 tablespoons fresh lemon juice
1 cup peeled, chopped	1 small clove garlic, pressed
cucumber	

Combine all ingredients in saucepan, bring just to boil, turn down heat, cover, and simmer 10 minutes. Remove from heat, and when cool, puree in blender. Serves 6-8.

☙ CREAM OF MUSHROOM SOUP ☙

A satisfying soup for snowy days, with rich and subtle flavoring. Fresh mushroom soup is a treat, no matter how you slice them. Include a ½-pint carton of whipping cream with the soup, along with written instructions advising that the soup should be reheated over low heat, and not reach boiling. The cream should be added just before serving.

CHICKEN STOCK

- 2 quarts water
- 2 pounds chicken necks, backs, and giblets
- 1 carrot, sliced
- 1 stalk celery, sliced
- 1 large onion, sliced
- 2 cloves garlic
- *bouquet garni* (sprig parsley, 1 bay leaf, ½ teaspoon thyme, and 4 peppercorns, all placed in a tea ball, or tied in cheesecloth)

In large stock pot, heat all stock ingredients to boiling; cover, and simmer 4 hours. Skim fat from surface; strain and discard bones, vegetables, and *bouquet garni.*

SOUP

- ¼ pound butter
- 1 pound mushrooms, sliced
- ½ teaspoon lemon juice
- ⅔ cup flour
- 2 quarts chicken stock
- 1 teaspoon salt
- pepper to taste

• • •

½-pint carton whipping cream

To make soup, melt butter over medium heat in heavy soup pot. Add mushrooms and lemon juice, stirring vigorously to coat mushrooms with butter. Reduce heat, cover, and cook over medium-low heat 20 minutes, stirring occasionally. Remove cover, and stir flour into mushrooms until smooth and bubbly. Add chicken stock and increase heat, stirring constantly until mixture is boiling. Cover and reduce heat to low; simmer 1 hour (or longer), stirring occasionally, until soup has thickened. Add salt and pepper to taste. Serves 6-8.

☙ ALMOST FRENCH PEA SOUP ❧

Once in a French restaurant, I was served the most exquisite pea soup the world has ever known. Sad to say, the chef wouldn't part with the recipe, so over the years I've worked at duplicating it. This recipe is close . . .

Pea soup always tastes better the second day, so if possible refrigerate overnight. It should be reheated gently, and it may be frozen. Corn muffins (page 56) go well with this soup. Most children seem to hate the very idea of pea soup, so give it to adults only.

1 pound dry green split peas	1 cup whipping cream
water to cover	1 teaspoon tarragon
1 ham bone	½ teaspoon marjoram
3 cloves garlic	1½ teaspoons sugar
2 medium onions, chopped	1 teaspoon salt
1 bay leaf	2 good shakes of pepper, or to
¼ teaspoon thyme	taste
1½ quarts water	1 cup diced ham

Soak peas in water to cover for 1 hour; drain. In heavy dutch oven, place peas, ham bone, garlic, onions, bay leaf, thyme, and 1½ quarts water. Cover, bring to boil, then simmer 3 hours. Remove bone and bay leaf; rub soup through a sieve (discard whatever doesn't go through). Return soup to low heat; stir in cream, seasonings, and ham. Serves 6.

☙ GOLDEN ONION SOUP ❧

My grandmother invented this soup — which, like her, has a French heritage and Spanish seasoning. Accompanying instructions should advise that this soup is to be reheated in a double boiler, over hot water.

4 cups cream	1 tablespoon flour
⅓ cup chicken broth	¼ teaspoon ground saffron
1 tablespoon cooking oil	threads
4 tablespoons butter	salt and pepper
3 large onions, thinly sliced	

Heat cream and chicken broth together in heavy saucepan, stirring often, just to steaming point — do not boil. Remove from heat and set aside. In soup pot, heat oil and butter, add onions, and cook slowly 15 minutes, or until golden. Stir frequently. Remove the onions and reserve. Stir flour into pot with a whisk, whisking continually for about 2 minutes. Add saffron, then slowly add cream and chicken broth mixture, stirring continually. When soup starts to thicken, add onions, and simmer gently 10 minutes. Season with salt and pepper. Serves 4.

✻ JOE'S CASTILIAN SEAFOOD STEW ✻

My father based this recipe on seafood soups served by his family in Madrid. A wonderful dish for a family reunion, but don't try to freeze it. Package the stew when cool in a leak-proof container large enough to hold 2 quarts — unless you decide to keep half for yourself; generosity has its limits. Send along a card giving the name of the recipe and instructions for its use. Emphasize that when this stew is reheated, it must not be boiled for more than 30 seconds.

1 cup finely chopped onions
1 green pepper, finely chopped
1 clove garlic, pressed
3 tomatoes, peeled, seeded, and chopped
2 medium potatoes, cut in ½-inch dice
4 carrots, thinly sliced
⅓ cup chopped parsley
½ teaspoon thyme
1 bay leaf
½ teaspoon salt
½ teaspoon pepper

fish stock
1½ cups dry white wine
1 pound each of two kinds firm, white fish (cod and pollock are good)
2 cups chopped clams (with canned clams, drain off most of the juice — ½ cup juice is plenty)
½ pound scallops
1 pound squid (cleaned and cut into 2-inch strips)

Fish Stock: My father boils two fish carcasses (obtained free from the local fish market) with salt and pepper in about a quart of water for 15 minutes, then strains off the stock, discarding the carcasses.

In 2-quart kettle, sauté onions, green pepper, and garlic in butter. Add tomatoes, potatoes, carrots, parsley, thyme, bay leaf, salt, pepper, and just enough fish stock to cover the vegetables; cover, and simmer 15 minutes. Then add wine, fish, clams, scallops, and squid; bring to boil, cover, and cook 5-10 minutes more, checking frequently as overcooking will toughen the clams and squid and make the other seafood mushy. Serves 8-12.

✻ SPINACH SOUP ✻

A rich, creamy soup distinguished by a tang of mustard and a hint of nutmeg. Include a plastic bag containing the two hardboiled eggs with the soup, along with written instructions advising that the soup should be heated just to the boiling point, and that the hardboiled eggs should be sliced over the top, just before serving.

1 medium onion, sliced thin
1 clove garlic, pressed
3 tablespoons butter
2 tablespoons flour
½ teaspoon dry mustard
¼ teaspoon nutmeg
1 teaspoon salt

¼ teaspoon pepper
10-ounce package frozen
  chopped spinach, thawed
2 cups cream
2 cups chicken stock
• • •
2 hardboiled eggs in shells

Sauté onion and garlic in butter. Blend in flour, mustard, nutmeg, salt, and pepper, stirring continually until smooth and bubbly. Stir in spinach. In separate saucepan, heat cream and stock together, then gradually pour into spinach mixture, stirring continually. Simmer gently 10 minutes. Serves 4.

✻ ZESTY TURKEY SOUP ✻

A recipe I invented one year when we had turkey for both Thanksgiving and Christmas; variations on the turkey soup theme were in order. This recipe may be frozen.

1 turkey carcass
1 quart water
2 cloves garlic
bouquet garni (bay leaf, 12
  peppercorns, 8 cloves in a tea
  ball or tied up in cheesecloth)

1½ cups egg or spinach noodles
3 carrots, thinly sliced on the
  diagonal
2 eggs
½ pound pepperoni, thinly
  sliced

Crack turkey bones, place carcass in water with garlic and *bouquet garni,* and cook 1 hour. Cool, and remove meat from bones; discard bones and *bouquet garni,* and return meat to broth. Add noodles, carrots, eggs in shells, and pepperoni. Bring to boil, cover, and cook for 15-20 minutes more. Remove eggs from broth, shell, and slice into soup. Serves 4-6.

✳ SPANISH VEGETABLE BEAN SOUP ✳

This was my grandmother's all-purpose soup — a base for whatever vegetables were in season, but always including the beans. This soup may be frozen, and is wonderful served with hot garlic bread.

½ pound pinto beans
¼ pound salt pork
1 quart water
1 large onion, chopped
2 cloves garlic, pressed
2 carrots, thinly sliced
2 green peppers, chopped
2 potatoes, peeled and cubed
whatever other vegetables
   are handy

1 teaspoon thyme
½ teaspoon red pepper seeds
2 garlic cloves, crushed
¼ pound chourico or other spicy
   sausage, cut in ¼-inch pieces
¼ pound lean ham or
   prosciutto, diced
3 cups dry red wine
salt and pepper

Soak beans overnight; drain. Place beans, salt pork, and water in soup pot. Cover, bring just to boil, then simmer 2 hours. Add vegetables, seasonings, sausage, ham, and wine; simmer 1 hour more. Discard salt pork, and season soup with salt and pepper to taste. Serves 8.

✳ TOMATO-LEEK SOUP ✳

Give this quick and easy soup in a thermos to friends about to embark on cold-weather activities. Include lemon slices in a plastic bag for garnish.

2 cups tomato juice
1½ cups (10½-ounce can)
   tomato puree
1 tablespoon brown sugar
1 teaspoon ground cloves
3 leeks, chopped (or 5 scallions),
   white parts only

2 cups beef stock
1 teaspoon salt
1 bay leaf
½ teaspoon thyme
• • •
1 lemon, thinly sliced

Combine all ingredients together in a soup kettle; cover, and simmer 45 minutes. Serves 6.

CASSEROLES AND ONE-DISH MEALS

The best gift casseroles, as I've learned from my own experience, are those which are a meal in themselves, and only require reheating. Minimum effort on the part of the donee should be the rule. The casseroles below fulfill these requirements and are just special enough to be received with joy.

℥ SPANISH MEATBALLS ℥

My grandmother used to serve these over mashed potatoes, but they are just as good over toast points. Smaller meatballs may be served in their sauce as a hot hors d'oeuvre. Have toothpicks handy. Written instructions accompanying this dish should advise to reheat gently in a double boiler, as boiling can curdle the gravy. Should this occur, it will not affect the flavor, just the appearance. Don't try to freeze it.

1 pound ground veal	1 quart water
½ pound ground pork	1 medium onion
½ cup grated cheese (Swiss or Monterey Jack)	1 clove garlic
	1 bay leaf
1 egg	pinch thyme
1 cup cracker crumbs	1 teaspoon salt
1 tablespoon fresh chopped marjoram or ½ teaspoon dried	dash pepper
	2 tablespoons olive oil
	2 egg yolks
salt and pepper to taste	1 tablespoon lemon juice

In a bowl, combine veal, pork, cheese, egg, cracker crumbs, marjoram, salt, and pepper; form into balls. Place water in pot; add onion, garlic clove, bay leaf, thyme, salt, pepper, and olive oil. Bring to boil, and drop in meatballs. Reduce heat, cover pot, and simmer 1 hour. Remove meatballs to deep dish, and cover to keep warm. Discard onion, garlic, and bay leaf. Reserve 2 cups of broth in pot. Beat egg yolks in a small bowl, and stir in a little of the boiling broth. Return this mixture to broth in pot. Simmer over medium heat, stirring constantly until thickened. Remove from heat and add lemon juice. Pour over meatballs. Serves 6-8.

❦ CASSOULET ❦

My French grandmother raised a family in Spain, and her cooking reflected both worlds. Sadly, only a few of her recipes have survived, as she cooked "by feel." This is one of hers — a hearty one-pot meal almost too good to give away.

The flavors of this dish are enhanced if it is refrigerated a day before giving. Reheat in 300°F. oven for 30 minutes; add more beef stock if it looks dry. This recipe will keep in the refrigerator up to 10 days, but does not freeze well. The perfect finishing touch would be a greens salad packed to accompany this dish.

1 pound dried pea (navy) beans
water to cover
4 cups beef stock
1 teaspoon salt
1 pound chourico, or Italian
  sausage
duckling giblets, chopped
¼ pound salt pork, diced
1 medium onion, chopped
6 cloves garlic, peeled and
  minced

2 large carrots, sliced
1½ cups tomato puree
½ teaspoon black pepper
1 pound smoked boneless ham,
  cooked and sliced
1 duckling, cut in pieces
5¾-ounce jar pimiento-stuffed
  olives, sliced

• • •

greens salad

Soak beans in water to cover overnight. Drain, and place in large pot with beef stock and salt. Cover, bring to boil; reduce heat, and simmer 20 minutes, or until skins burst when blown upon. Remove from heat and set aside. In large frying pan, brown sausage and giblets; add salt pork. When salt pork is browned, add onion, garlic, and carrots; cook about 15 minutes, or until tender. Blend in tomato puree and pepper, and heat through. Add this mixture and the ham to the beans. Mix well, and bring to boil. Cover, turn down heat, and simmer 2 hours, stirring occasionally.

Meanwhile, rinse duckling pieces with cold water, pat dry, and place skin-side-down on rack in shallow roasting pan. Cook at 350°F. for 1½ hours, or until done. Brush with drippings occasionally, and turn with tongs.

Remove bean mixture from heat and ladle one third of the beans into a 5-quart pot. Cover with a layer of olives, pork, sausage, and duckling (using about half of each). Repeat layers, ending with beans, and topping with several slices of chourico or Italian sausage. Heat at 350°F. for 1 hour. Serves 8.

⚜ *ARROZ CON POLLO* ⚜

A good friend liked to call this dish "A Rose cone Polio," which I'm sure caused my linguist grandfather to roll in his grave. No matter how you pronounce its name, this dish is superb eating. Make it for yourself first, and you'll see. Like the Cassoulet (page 25), this is one of the few of my grandmother's recipes which was written down. Send along with a tossed green salad to make a perfect meal. Do not freeze.

1 chicken, cut in pieces
3 tablespoons olive oil
1 large onion, chopped
1 clove garlic, pressed
2 cups water
1 large bay leaf (or 2 small)
pinch thyme
salt and pepper to taste
2 cups water
1 medium onion, whole
1 bay leaf

inch thyme
½ pound fresh shrimp in shells
10-ounce can baby clams
4-ounce jar pimiento, drained
   and cut in strips
1 pint clam juice
¼ teaspoon ground saffron
   threads
3 cups (more or less) uncooked
   long-grain rice

In large frying pan, brown chicken pieces in olive oil; remove chicken and set aside. In same oil, sauté chopped onion and garlic. Return chicken to pan with 2 cups of water, bay leaf, thyme, salt, and pepper. Cover, and simmer 40 minutes, or until chicken is tender. Meanwhile, in medium saucepan, bring 2 cups water, whole onion, bay leaf, and second pinch of thyme to boil. Cover pan, turn down heat, and cook until onion is soft. Add shrimp in shells and cook 10 minutes more. Remove shrimp, discard onion and bay leaf, and reserve broth. Add shrimp to chicken (my grandmother never shelled or deveined her shrimp, but you may prefer to), along with baby clams, pimientoes, clam juice, and saffron. Add reserved shrimp broth. Measure all liquid in pan, and add half as much rice. Bring to boil and let boil for 2-3 minutes, stirring so it won't stick.

At this point my grandmother would transfer everything to a large covered roasting pan, which she baked at 350°F. in the oven, shaking the pan every 10 minutes or so to separate the grains of rice. It took about 45 minutes for the rice to be done. Perhaps because I'm third generation, I do it the easier way, and cook the chicken, shrimp, etc. and rice in the original covered frying pan, on top of the stove, over low heat, for 25 minutes. However my *arroz* is always a little sticky, and hers *never* was. Serves 8.

⚓ CHICKEN POT PIE ⚓

Nothing more down-home than homemade chicken pot pie!
Wonderful for sick or homesick friends. Accompanying
instructions should advise reheating in 300°F. oven for 20
minutes. Does not freeze well.

3½- to 4-pound chicken with
  giblets, including gizzard and
  neck
6 cups water
3 large carrots, peeled and
  trimmed
1 stalk celery with leaves
1 small onion
1 bay leaf
pinch thyme
6 tablespoons butter

16-ounce jar boiled onions,
  drained
half a 10-ounce package frozen
  peas, or ¾ cup fresh peas
4 tablespoons flour
1½ cups cream, room
  temperature
½ teaspoon dry mustard
salt and pepper to taste
pinch tarragon
plain pastry (page 65)

Rinse chicken, cut in quarters, and remove fat. Place in stock pot with giblets, water, carrots, celery, onion, bay leaf, and thyme. Bring to boil, cover, turn down heat, and simmer 2 hours; cool in broth. Reserve broth and carrots, discard celery, onion, bay leaf, gizzard, and neck. Skin and bone chicken, cutting up remaining giblets and meat into bite-size pieces. Measure 3 cups of broth (reserve remainder for other use), and boil, uncovered, until reduced by half. Set aside. Slice carrots.

Melt 2 tablespoons butter in medium frying pan, stir in onions, peas, and sliced carrots. Cook over low heat 5 minutes, then add chicken meat. Remove from heat, cover, and set aside.

In heavy saucepan, heat remaining 4 tablespoons butter, stir in flour, and cook over low heat until smooth and bubbly, stirring constantly. Add reduced chicken broth slowly, increasing heat while stirring constantly until mixture is thick and smooth. Then reduce heat again, and stir in cream; cook 5 minutes over low heat, stirring frequently. Season with mustard, salt, pepper, and tarragon. Pour sauce over vegetables and chicken, and let cool.

Butter a deep 3-quart baking dish, and spoon chicken mixture into it. Roll out pastry and fit over top of baking dish, pressing edges against the rim. Slash pastry to vent. Bake at 375°F. for 35-40 minutes. Serves 6.

⚜ CURRIED CHICKEN ⚜

An uncomplicated, mildly curried East Indian dish; send a jar of Major Stone's Chutney (page 135) along with it.

1 chicken, cut in pieces	¾ teaspoon sugar
1 tablespoon vegetable oil	¼ teaspoon ground ginger
3 tablespoons butter	1 cup chicken broth
1 small onion, chopped	1 cup sour cream
1½ teaspoons curry powder	1 cup long-grained rice
3 tablespoons flour	• • •
¾ teaspoon salt	*chutney*

In heavy dutch oven, brown chicken pieces in oil and butter. Remove chicken, and sauté onion and curry powder. Blend in flour, salt, sugar, and ginger, and cook over low heat until mixture is smooth and bubbly. Remove from heat. Stir in chicken broth and sour cream. Boil 1 minute, stirring constantly. Add chicken pieces, cover, and cook over low heat 30 minutes. Add rice and cook slowly 15 minutes more. Serves 4.

⚜ CHILI ⚜

There are surely no two chili recipes alike, and everyone who makes it from scratch claims his or hers is the best. However, they're wrong; this *is the best. Include a bag of corn chips and plastic bag of grated cheese, along with instructions indicating that the heated chili should be served over the corn chips, and topped with the cheese.*

1 pound lean hamburger	1 teaspoon salt
2 onions, chopped	⅛ teaspoon cayenne, or to taste
1 green pepper, chopped	1-2 tablespoons chili powder
2 cloves garlic, pressed	1 teaspoon cinnamon
2 tablespoons shortening	• • •
20-ounce can tomatoes	*corn chips*
6-ounce can tomato paste	*sharp Cheddar cheese, coarsely*
15-ounce can kidney beans, drained	*grated*

In heavy dutch oven, sauté hamburger, onions, pepper, and garlic in melted shortening. Add other ingredients, bring to boil, cover, turn down heat, and simmer 3 hours or more, stirring occasionally. Serves 6.

✕ FISH CASSEROLE ✕

Fish in a sherried cheese sauce with mushrooms makes an elegant gift dish for seafood lovers. Accompanying instructions should caution not to overheat upon reheating — bake 10 minutes at 300°F. in dish covered with aluminum wrap.

2 pounds haddock or other firm white fish, cut up	dash pepper
water to cover	2 cups milk
1 bay leaf	1 cup grated Swiss cheese
pinch thyme	⅓ cup sherry
4 tablespoons butter	4 tablespoons butter
4 tablespoons flour	3 cups sliced mushrooms
½ teaspoon salt	¾ cup fine bread crumbs
	4 tablespoons butter, melted

In large saucepan, place fish and water, with bay leaf and thyme. Cover, bring just to boil; reduce heat, and simmer gently 10 minutes, or until fish turns white and flakes easily. Remove fish from water and flake; set aside. Reserve water, and discard bay leaf.

Make a white sauce: in a heavy saucepan, melt first 4 tablespoons butter over low heat. Blend in flour, salt, and pepper, stirring until mixture is smooth and bubbly. Gradually stir in milk, and bring to boil. Let boil 1 minute, stirring constantly, until sauce has thickened. Reduce heat. Stir in ½ cup of water in which fish was cooked, then the cheese. When sauce is smooth, add sherry, stirring until sauce is uniform. Remove from heat.

In heavy saucepan, melt 4 tablespoons butter, and sauté mushrooms over medium high heat 2-3 minutes. Place fish in buttered, 7x11-inch baking dish, top with mushrooms, and pour cheese sauce over all. Sprinkle with crumbs, and drizzle 4 tablespoons melted butter over top. Bake at 350°F. for 30 minutes, or until bubbly. Be careful not to overcook, as sauce may curdle. Serves 6.

⚠ POOR MAN'S LASAGNA ⚠

Use elbow macaroni in this dish, or dress it up with old-fashioned egg noodles. It's amazing the difference a noodle shape can make. This casserole freezes well.

3 cups egg noodles, or macaroni of your choice
water to cook them in
1 medium onion, chopped fine
1 green pepper, chopped fine
1½ pounds hamburger

two 8-ounce cans tomato sauce
1 envelope dried onion soup mix
1 cup cottage cheese
8-ounce package cream cheese
1 cup sour cream

Cook and drain egg noodles. Brown onion, pepper, and hamburger; add tomato sauce and onion soup mix. In separate bowl, mix both cheeses with sour cream. Put half the noodles in buttered 2-quart casserole, cover with cheese mixture, and top with remaining egg noodles. Pour meat mixture over top. Cover, and bake at 375°F. for 45 minutes. Serves 6.

⚠ MEAT PIE ⚠

This pie is versatile — good for breakfast, lunch, or supper. For a nice extra touch enclose a bottle of homemade barbecue sauce (page 134) as a condiment with pie. Reheat at 300°F. for 20 minutes. May be frozen.

1 medium onion, chopped
1 clove garlic, pressed
2 tablespoons olive oil
1 potato, peeled and sliced
½ pound lean hamburger
½ pound sausage meat
¼ cup water

¼ teaspoon sage
pinch ground cloves
salt and pepper
3 tablespoons butter
plain pastry (page 65)

• • •

barbecue sauce

In large frying pan, sauté onion and garlic in olive oil; then add potato, hamburger, and sausage, to brown. Add water and all seasonings, cover, and simmer 30 minutes. Skim fat from broth, and with a potato masher, mash ingredients together, adding butter. Set aside.

Make pastry. Roll out bottom pie crust, and lay in a 9- or 10-inch pie pan. Add meat filling. Roll out top crust, fit over top, and seal edges. Slash top crust to vent. Bake at 375°F. for 45 minutes, or until crust is golden. Serves 6.

⚜ ITALIAN MEATBALLS AND SAUCE ⚜

My mother-in-law gave me this recipe — the perfect gift for large families or gatherings, it feeds twelve at least, and is a real crowd pleaser. Perfect for a church supper. If you give it as a gift, send a box of spaghetti and a jug of Chianti wine, a loaf of French or Italian bread wrapped in foil or in a plastic bag, and a bag of hand-grated Romano or Parmesan cheese along with it.

SAUCE

1 pound Italian sausage, mild or hot, cut in 1-inch chunks
2 tablespoons olive oil
1 medium onion, chopped
2 cloves garlic, pressed
two 6-ounce cans tomato paste

28-ounce can Italian tomatoes
2 bay leaves
dash oregano
½ teaspoon basil
salt and pepper to taste

MEATBALLS

1½ pounds hamburger
1 cup seasoned bread crumbs
½ cup grated Parmesan or Romano cheese
1 tablespoon chopped fresh parsley
½ teaspoon garlic salt
pepper to taste

½ cup milk
2 beaten eggs

• • •

16-ounce box spaghetti
Chianti wine
fresh French or Italian bread
hand-grated Romano or Parmesan cheese

To make sauce, in 6-quart dutch oven brown sausage in olive oil. When browned, remove sausage, pour off all but 2-3 tablespoons of fat, and sauté onion and garlic in remaining fat. Return sausage to pot, along with tomato paste, tomatoes, and seasonings. Cover, bring to boil, reduce heat, and simmer several hours, stirring once every ½ hour to prevent sticking. Italian sauce tastes better the longer it is cooked; this one is especially good aged overnight.

When tomatoes have cooked down to a uniformly thick consistency, it is time to make the meatballs. Combine all ingredients, mixing with your fingers. Form into balls and drop into simmering sauce. Cover and simmer gently 1 hour more, stirring every 15 minutes. (Meatballs are apt to stick, especially on electric stoves or in a thin pot.) Serves 12.

☙ PAT BELDEN'S FRENCH ONION PIE ☙

A simple-minded quiche both easy and tasty. Make one in a disposable foil pan to give away, another in a pie pan for home use. Accompanying instructions should advise that the quiche be covered with foil before reheating at 300°F. Do not freeze.

PASTRY *(makes two 9- or 10-inch pie shells)*

2 cups flour	¾ cup vegetable shortening
1 teaspoon salt	3-4 tablespoons cold water

PIE *(fills one 9- or 10-inch pie shell)*

3½-ounce can (2 cups) French-fried onions	1½ cups shredded sharp Cheddar cheese
4 eggs	½ teaspoon salt
1½ cups milk	dash cayenne

To prepare pastry, sift flour and salt into bowl. Cut in shortening with pastry blender or two knives to the size of peas. Sprinkle cold water over mixture (I use a laundry sprinkler with a removable perforated top), mixing with a fork until it holds together. Using a floured pastry cloth and covered rolling pin (I use an old sock), roll out half the dough. Press pastry into pie pan and flute edges. (Roll out other half of dough, press in pie pan, seal in plastic bag, and freeze for future use. Or better yet, make another pie for yourself.) Pierce bottom crust several times with a fork, and bake for 7-8 minutes in 450°F. oven, or until golden. Reduce oven to 325°F. Line warm pastry shell with 1½ cups French-fried onions. Beat eggs slightly, blend in milk, ½ cup shredded cheese, and seasonings; pour over onions. Sprinkle remaining shredded cheese on top. Bake at 325°F. for 45 minutes. Sprinkle remaining onions over top of pie, and bake 5-10 minutes more. A knife inserted in the center should come out clean. Serves 6.

⚔ PAELLA ⚔

Paella is essentially a more elaborate Arroz con Pollo, subject to the personal interpretation of its creator. I've had paellas with lobster, langostinos, squid, chunks of ham, and any number of vegetables — all terrific. Here's mine.

A paella doesn't need much by way of accompaniment, but a jug of good rosé wine and a loaf of bread would win you fans for life. Reheat, covered, over low heat.

1 chicken, cut in pieces
3 tablespoons olive oil
½ pound chorizo, chourico, or other garlic-seasoned pork sausage, sliced in bite-size pieces
1 large onion, chopped
2 cloves garlic, pressed
2 cups uncooked long-grain rice
4 cups chicken broth
1 tablespoon tomato paste
1 large bay leaf

½ teaspoon thyme
¼ teaspoon ground saffron threads
salt and pepper to taste
8 little-neck clams, washed
8 mussels, washed
10-ounce package frozen green peas

• • •

rosé wine
loaf of fresh bread

In 2-quart dutch oven, brown chicken in olive oil; remove chicken and set aside. In same oil, brown sausage, then onion and garlic; remove all, and place with chicken. Stir rice into oil and brown lightly. Remove rice and set aside. Return chicken, sausage, onion, and garlic to pan. Add chicken broth, tomato paste, bay leaf, thyme, saffron, salt, and pepper. Bring just to boil, cover, reduce heat, and simmer 40 minutes, or until chicken is tender. Add the browned rice, clams, and mussels; bring to boil again, cover, reduce heat, and simmer 20 minutes or until liquid is absorbed. (If you have a paella dish, assemble ingredients in it and cook on stove top over low heat, or in 300°F. oven until liquid is absorbed.) Sprinkle frozen peas over the top during last few minutes of cooking time. Serves 8.

✙ PORK KAROKI ✙

I've always loved to enter recipe contests. Amazingly, I win something occasionally — this recipe earned me a gas grill. Instructions should advise that this dish may be reheated over low heat, or in a 325°F. oven. Fluff up rice before serving.

MARINADE

⅔ cup corn syrup
2 tablespoons cider vinegar
1 clove garlic, pressed

1 teaspoon salt
½ teaspoon dried rosemary

PORK

1 pound center-cut pork fillets,
   cut in strips
3 tablespoons olive oil
1 ounce slivered almonds
1½ cups boiling water

2 chicken bouillon cubes
10-ounce package frozen
   artichoke hearts
¾ cup uncooked long-grained
   rice

Prepare marinade by combining all ingredients 6 hours before serving. Pour over pork strips, cover dish, and set in refrigerator to marinate, turning meat occasionally. After 6-12 hours, remove pork from marinade and drain on paper towels. Reserve marinade. In dutch oven, brown pork in olive oil, then add slivered almonds, and cook 2-3 minutes more. Add boiling water, bouillon cubes, artichoke hearts, and 2 tablespoons of marinade. Return to boil, cover, reduce heat, and simmer 10 minutes. Stir in rice, cover, and simmer 20 minutes more. Serves 4.

✙ SPANAKOPITA ✙

The perfect gift meal for vegetarians. Written instructions should advise to reheat in 300°F. oven, and to cut in squares for serving.

1 pound filo (phyllo) pastry
   (about 12-15 sheets)
1 pound fresh spinach, or two
   10-ounce packages frozen
   spinach, thawed
1 pound feta cheese

½ teaspoon salt
pinch nutmeg
6 eggs, beaten
½ cup cooking oil
¼ pound butter, melted

Defrost filo 2 hours ahead. Wash and steam fresh spinach 5 minutes, or cook frozen spinach according to package instructions. Drain spinach, fresh or frozen, thoroughly, and place in bowl. Crumble in cheese, mix in salt, nutmeg, and eggs, and set aside. Heat oil and butter in small pan; unwrap filo and smooth out creases. Plan to use half the filo sheets for the bottom layers, and half for the top layers. (Keep filo pastry covered with damp paper towel while working, as it dries easily, and crumbles.) Oil bottom and sides of rectangular 9x13-inch baking pan. Lay one sheet of pastry in pan, letting it overlap the sides, and dribble with warm oil/butter mixture. Top with sheet of filo pastry, and dribble with oil/butter mixture again. Continue in this fashion until half of the filo sheets are used. Spread spinach, cheese, and egg mixture over the filo layers, then cover with remaining filo layers, dribbling oil/butter mixture between each sheet as before. Trim excess pastry, leaving about a 1-inch margin. Tuck this in around the inside edges of the pan. Brush top and edges with remaining oil/butter mixture. Bake at 350°F. for 50 minutes. Serves 6-8.

❦ VEAL PARMIGIANA ❦

I've used this recipe so long and so often that the recipe card is barely legible. It's simple to make, and popular with both kids and adults. This recipe may be frozen in freezer container.

3 tablespoons vegetable oil	½ cup grated Parmesan cheese
1 small onion, chopped	½ cup bread crumbs
1 clove garlic, pressed	6 slices (1 pound) veal cutlets
two 8-ounce cans tomato sauce	1 egg, beaten
¼ cup water	¼ cup vegetable oil
1 teaspoon oregano	8-ounce package sliced
⅛ teaspoon black pepper	mozzarella cheese
1 tablespoon chopped fresh	2 tablespoons grated Parmesan
parsley	cheese

In heavy saucepan heat oil; sauté onion and garlic in oil until golden. Stir in tomato sauce, water, oregano, pepper, and parsley. Cover, and simmer 10 minutes. Meanwhile, combine ½ cup Parmesan cheese and bread crumbs. Dip veal slices in beaten egg, then in cheese/crumb mixture. Heat oil in dutch oven, and sauté veal until golden. Remove veal, drain oil, and pour half the tomato sauce over bottom of dutch oven. Place veal on top, then mozzarella slices. Pour remaining sauce over this, and sprinkle with Parmesan cheese. Cover, and bake at 350°F. for 30 minutes. Serves 6.

VEAL SCALLOPINI

Reheat at 300°F. for 20 minutes, but don't try to freeze, as it will become dry.

MARINADE

1 teaspoon salt
2 teaspoons paprika
½ cup cooking oil
juice of 1 lemon
1 clove garlic, pressed
1 teaspoon Dijon mustard
½ teaspoon sugar
¼ teaspoon nutmeg

VEAL

6-8 veal cutlets
¾ cup flour
pinch salt
2 tablespoons butter
1 tablespoon oil
1 cup sliced mushrooms
12 pimiento-stuffed olives, sliced
1 cup chicken stock

Combine marinade ingredients. Place veal in pan or bowl, and pour marinade over it. Marinate 1 hour, turning once. Remove veal; reserve marinade. Shake marinated veal in a paper bag with flour and salt; then brown cutlets in melted butter/oil mixture in frying pan. Place cutlets in dutch oven with mushrooms, olives, chicken stock, and half the marinade. Cover and bake at 300°F. for 1 hour. Serves 6-8.

SUSANN'S VERMICELLI CASSEROLE

Unlike most carbonaras, this one reheats well in heavy saucepan over low heat. Good for friends who need fattening up.

¼ to ⅓ box vermicelli
boiling water to cook it in
2 eggs
2 egg yolks
1 cup freshly grated Parmesan cheese
1 cup chopped fresh parsley
½ teaspoon garlic salt
salt and pepper to taste
8 thick slices bacon
1 pint heavy cream
4 tablespoons butter

Place vermicelli in boiling water; cook until just tender. Drain and keep hot. In medium bowl, mix eggs, egg yolks, cheese, parsley, and seasonings; set aside. In large frying pan, fry bacon until crisp. Drain on paper towel. Discard all but 1 tablespoon of bacon fat. Add cream, butter, and vermicelli; then egg/cheese mixture. Cook over medium heat, stirring continually, until eggs are just done. Crumble bacon over top and stir. Serves 6.

⚡ *CHAPTER 2* ⚡
Yeast Breads and Rolls, Quick Breads and Muffins

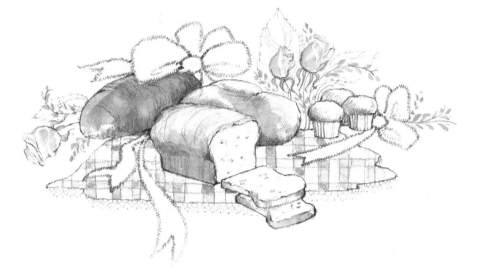

*B*reads are perhaps the most traditional of kitchen gifts. There are special breads to bake for all sorts of occasions, depending on ethnic and religious customs. But freshly baked breads are always welcome — a symbol of friendship and hospitality worldwide.

Flour is essential to breadmaking. Use the best you can find. Where white flour is called for, I recommend the unbleached kind, because of its higher gluten content. In New England you're most likely to find it under the trademark of "King Arthur," or "Robin Hood." Elsewhere look for the description "unbleached." All of the breads here (except where noted) can be frozen. Make sure that any bread to be frozen is thoroughly cooled, otherwise condensation inside the freezer wrap will make the outside of the bread soggy when thawed.

As to storage: yeast breads can be kept out on the counter (wrap in plastic wrap or aluminum foil) for three to four days. Refrigerate wrapped quick breads after the first day.

PACKAGING YEAST BREADS AND ROLLS, QUICK BREADS AND MUFFINS

In packaging these items, the prime object is to preserve freshness. Therefore, the first step is to wrap the cooled loaves, rolls, or muffins, individually, in plastic wrap* or aluminum foil. For hand delivery, place muffins or rolls in a foil pan, itself wrapped in foil or plastic. Loaves need only the first wrapping. Tie up with a bit of ribbon, and attach card (see below). For mailing, tin boxes, found in all shapes, sizes, and decorative motifs at kitchen-accessory shops, or specialty shops, are super containers. You can be sure the item will arrive whole. Tin boxes are both airtight, and sturdy — a particular advantage when mailing food. And when the bread is gone, they make nice countertop storage containers. (Do not refrigerate, as they may rust.)

Another handsome way to present breads, rolls, or muffins, is in an attractive, reusable basket which may contain just one food gift or (see cover) an assortment. Inexpensive, colorful kerchiefs make a nice basket liner. Breadboards and fancy trays may also be sent with the wrapped loaf, rolls, or muffins. Or include a cooking utensil — measuring cups, measuring spoons, whisk, wooden spoon, etc.

Instructions for reheating and serving should be written out on a card or square of colored construction paper (verbal instructions are apt to be forgotten), along with other pertinent information: i.e., whether the item has already been frozen, whether it may be frozen, etc. Punch a hole in the instruction card and tie card on with ribbon, or affix solidly with tape, so it won't become detached and lost.

All the foods in this chapter (except Cream Cheese Coffee Cake) are appropriate for mailing. Bake quick breads in disposable foil loaf pan, take them from pan and cool on rack. Wash and dry pan; wrap cooled bread in foil, and replace in pan. Mail right in the pan — good for added support. Mail in a tin box or in a corrugated cardboard carton, using plenty of packing such as crunched-up newspaper, crushed styrofoam, plastic bubbles, or popcorn.

Seal mailing box with pressure-sensitive tape, and send package first-class, or by UPS whenever possible, to assure freshness.

These instructions are, in the main, also applicable to mailing cakes (Chapter 4) and other mailable foods.

*Because plastic wrap "breathes," do not use for items to be mailed.

YEAST BREADS AND ROLLS

✕ ANADAMA BREAD ✕

*The old New England favorite that Pepperidge Farm has made
famous.*

2 cups boiling water
1 cup corn meal
2 packages dry yeast
1 cup warm water

2 teaspoons salt
¼ pound butter, melted
½ cup molasses
5+ cups flour

In large bowl, slowly pour boiling water over corn meal,
stirring continually to avoid lumps. Let cool 1 hour. Dissolve
yeast in warm water, then add to corn meal along with other
ingredients. Mix thoroughly, cover, and let rise until doubled.
Turn out on floured board, knead 5 minutes, then divide and
shape into two loaves. Place in buttered 7x4-inch loaf pans, and
let rise again until doubled. Bake at 350°F. for 35 minutes.
Makes two 7-inch loaves.

❧ BREAKFAST BREAD ❧

A fine and nourishing gift for natural food fans.

1 cup uncooked corn meal
1 cup uncooked Maltex cereal
1 cup rolled oats
4 cups boiling water
2 packages dry yeast
½ cup warm water

½ cup molasses
½ cup packed brown sugar
2 teaspoons salt
2 cups whole wheat flour
6-8 cups white flour

Place corn meal, Maltex, and rolled oats in large bowl. Add boiling water and mix well. Let cool 1 hour. Dissolve yeast in warm water, then stir into cereal with molasses, sugar, and salt. Stir in whole wheat flour a little at a time, then gradually add white flour until dough is stiff and kneadable. Turn out on floured board, and knead 5 minutes (breads with whole wheat flour take more kneading to release the gluten). Place dough in greased bowl and turn to grease all surfaces. Cover and let rise until doubled. Punch down, shape into three loaves, and place in buttered 7x4-inch loaf pans. Let rise again in pans until doubled. Bake at 350°F. for 40-50 minutes. (To test for doneness, tap loaf bottom for a hollow sound.) Makes three 7-inch loaves.

❧ BUTTERMILK BREAD ❧

A faint maple flavor distinguishes this chewy bread.

2 packages dry yeast
½ cup warm water
2 tablespoons maple syrup
2 cups whole wheat flour

2-3 cups unbleached flour
2 teaspoons salt
2 tablespoons butter, melted
1½ cups buttermilk

Combine yeast, warm water, maple syrup, and set aside. In large bowl, mix flours, salt, melted butter, and buttermilk together, then add yeast mixture. Turn out on floured board, and knead until dough is smooth and elastic. Place dough in greased bowl, turn to grease evenly, cover, and let rise until doubled. Punch down, and form into two medium loaves. Place in buttered 7x4-inch loaf pans, cover with towel, and let rise again until doubled. Bake at 375°F. for 35-40 minutes. Makes two 7-inch loaves.

CREAM CHEESE COFFEE CAKE

A deluxe coffee cake perfect for wedding brunches, or other grand occasions. This recipe should not be frozen. If a Christmas offering, enclose a sprig of holly. Accompanying instructions should advise that ring should be refrigerated until used, and reheated at 300°F. With gift, include unopened jar of currant jam or jelly, and confectioners' sugar in a sandwich bag. When ready to serve, recipient should warm the red currant jam or jelly, stir well, and pour over ring for glaze, then sprinkle with confectioners' sugar.

2 packages dry yeast
½ cup warm water
5 cups sifted flour
1¼ cups sugar
½ teaspoon salt
6 egg yolks
1 cup sour cream
½ pound butter, melted

two 8-ounce packages cream
   cheese
2 whole eggs
1 teaspon vanilla

• • •

10-ounce jar red currant jam or
   jelly
½ cup sifted confectioners' sugar

Dissolve yeast in warm water, set aside. In large bowl, sift flour again with ¾ cup sugar and salt. In separate bowl, beat egg yolks until thick and light; blend in sour cream and melted butter. Stir in dissolved yeast. Gradually stir egg-yolk mixture into dry ingredients, making a soft, smooth dough. Turn onto floured board, and knead 5 minutes. Return to bowl, cover, and let rise until doubled.

Meanwhile, prepare cheese filling: beat cream cheese until light, then beat in remaining sugar. Add whole eggs, one at a time; beat until smooth. Add vanilla.

Punch down risen dough, and knead 3-4 minutes. Roll out dough on lightly floured board into circle about 18 inches in diameter. Lay 18-inch round of dough over greased 9- or 10-inch tube pan. Punch down dough into mold, fitting carefully so as not to tear, and allow it to hang over edges of pan. Cut cross in dough over center hole. Pour in cheese filling, and cover with overlapping outside and center edges. Let rise again until doubled. Bake at 350°F. for 30-40 minutes (30 minutes for 9-inch ring) or until cheese filling has set (knife inserted should come out clean). Cool 10 minutes in pan, and turn out on plate. Makes one 9- or 10-inch ring. Serves 8.

⚥ JUDY'S COFFEE CAN BREAD ⚥

A festive holiday bread. Bake in two 1-pound coffee cans, or one 2-pound coffee can. You can freeze this bread.

1 package dry yeast	1 teaspoon salt
½ cup warm water	2 tablespoons vegetable oil
⅛ teaspoon ground ginger	1 cup currants or candied fruit,
3 tablespoons sugar	or mixture of both
13-ounce can evaporated milk	4 cups flour (about)

In large bowl, dissolve yeast in warm water. Blend in ginger, and 1 tablespoon sugar. Let stand in warm place until bubbly — about 15 minutes. Stir in remaining 2 tablespoons sugar, milk, salt, vegetable oil, and currants or fruit. With mixer on low speed, blend in flour, 1 cup at a time, beating well after each addition. Beat in last cup of flour with spoon, if too stiff for mixer. Place dough in two greased 1-pound coffee cans, or one 2-pound coffee can. Cover each can with greased plastic lid. Let stand in warm place until plastic lid pops off. Discard lid, and bake 40-45 minutes at 350°F. for 1-pound cans, and 55-60 minutes for 2-pound can. Remove loaf or loaves from can(s) to cool on rack. Makes 1 large, or 2 medium cylindrical loaves.

⚥ ITALIAN EASTER EGG BRAID ⚥

Made with or without the eggs that can be cooked right in the bread as it bakes, this rich, fine-textured bread is very special. Freezes well, if made without the eggs-in-their-shells.

2 packages dry yeast	¼ pound butter, melted
2½ cups warm water	4 eggs, beaten
6 tablespoons sugar	8-9 cups all-purpose flour
2 teaspoons salt	(4 eggs in their shells)

In large bowl, dissolve yeast in warm water. Add sugar, salt, butter, beaten eggs, and 6 cups flour. Beat thoroughly with a wooden spoon. Gradually add remaining flour until dough is too stiff to beat. Turn out on floured board, and knead until smooth and elastic, adding more flour if dough is sticky. Return dough to large buttered bowl, turn to coat, cover, and let rise until doubled. For loaves: divide dough into twelve chunks, roll each chunk into a rope, and braid into four loaves. Place in four buttered 7x4-inch loaf pans. For Easter Braids: divide dough into six chunks, form six ropes, and braid into larger, flatter loaves. Place loaves on greased cookie sheets, and press two uncooked eggs (in their shells) into top of each loaf. Bake four loaf pans at 375°F. for 25-30 minutes. Bake braids on cookie sheets at 350°F. for 25-30 minutes. Makes four 7-inch loaves or 2 braids.

✕ LOUISE GREENE'S FINNISH COFFEE BREAD ✕

Our first loaf of this wondrously aromatic bread came as a house gift. It was such a hit — especially as toast at breakfast — that we begged the recipe, and appropriated it for our own.

BREAD

1 package dry yeast	½ teaspoon crushed or
¼ cup warm water	powdered cardamom
1 cup evaporated milk (room	2 eggs, lightly beaten
temperature)	4-4½ cups flour
1½ (or less) cups sugar	4 tablespoons butter, melted
½ teaspoon salt	

GLAZE

1 egg yolk, beaten	(¼ cup blanched almonds)
2 tablespoons milk	

In large bowl, dissolve yeast in warm water. Stir in milk, sugar, salt, cardamom, eggs, and 2 cups flour. Beat in butter until mix is smooth and glossy. Stir in enough flour to make dough easy to handle. Cover and let rest for 15 minutes.

Turn onto floured board; knead until smooth and elastic. Place in greased bowl, turn to grease evenly, cover, and let rise until doubled. Punch down, form loaves, and place in two well-greased 7x4-inch loaf pans. Let rise again until doubled. Preheat oven to 375°F. Mix glaze, and brush on loaves just before they go into the oven. Bake 20 minutes, or until light brown. Remove from pans, and cool on wire racks. Makes two 7-inch loaves.

✍ JUDY'S NEVER-FAIL OATMEAL BREAD ✍

Though I have always loved homemade bread, for years I never dared to make it. The mystique of baking intimidated me until my sister finally set me down with a training lump of her oatmeal bread dough. I found that even from scratch it was surprisingly easy — a truly no-fail recipe. Just be sure to use unbleached white flour. This bread is great fresh or toasted.

3 cups boiling water	¼ cup warm (105°F.) water
2 cups rolled oats	8 cups unbleached white flour,
1 teaspoon salt	or 4 cups unbleached white
1 cup molasses	flour plus 4 cups whole wheat
3 packages dry yeast	flour

In large bowl, pour boiling water over oatmeal and let stand 1 hour. Add salt, molasses, and yeast which has been dissolved in warm water. Stir in flour slowly until dough becomes quite stiff; turn out on floured board and knead remaining flour in by hand. Place in buttered bowl, turn to coat evenly, cover with plastic wrap, and let rise until doubled in a warm — but not hot — place (usually takes about 3 hours). Punch down, transfer to floured board and knead for at least 5 minutes, or until smooth and elastic. Divide dough equally for two large loaves (9x5 inches), or into three parts for three medium loaves (7x4 inches). Form each piece into a loaf and place in buttered loaf pans. Cover with towel, and let rise again until doubled. Bake at 375°F. until tops begin to brown; then turn down to 350°F. Bread will be baked in 40-50 minutes, depending upon size of loaves. Let cool in pans for 5 minutes, then gently disengage from pans and finish cooling on rack. Makes two 9-inch or three 7-inch loaves.

❧ PORTUGUESE SWEET BREAD ❧

Where I grew up in Rhode Island, you could buy Portuguese sweet bread hot from the oven at any corner bakery. Not so in New Hampshire, so I prevailed upon Dorothy Oliveira to give me her recipe to tide me over between visits to the home state.

3 packages dry yeast
1 cup warm water
7-8 cups white flour
2 cups sugar
½ teaspoon salt
6 eggs, well beaten

1 cup lukewarm evaporated milk
¼ pound butter, melted
2 teaspoons vanilla
(milk for glaze)

Dissolve yeast in warm water, and set aside. Sift flour, sugar, and salt together in large bowl. Add eggs, evaporated milk, melted butter, vanilla, and dissolved yeast. Knead together in bowl, adding more flour if necessary, until dough is stiff and elastic. Place in greased bowl and turn to coat all surfaces. Cover, and let rise until doubled. Divide into two round, flat loaves, and place in greased 8- or 9-inch square pans. Let rise again until doubled. To glaze, brush milk over loaves before baking. Bake at 325°F. for 30-35 minutes. Makes 2 round loaves.

❧ RAISIN ENGLISH MUFFIN BREAD ❧

A breakfast or tea bread at its best toasted, buttered, and served with homemade jam.

5-6 cups flour
2 packages dry yeast
2 tablespoons sugar
1 teaspoon cinnamon
2 teaspoons salt

¼ teaspoon baking soda
1 cup raisins
2 cups milk
½ cup water
corn meal

In large bowl, combine 3 cups flour, yeast, sugar, cinnamon, salt, baking soda, and raisins. Heat milk and water to lukewarm; add to dry ingredients, mixing well. Stir in remaining flour, and turn out onto floured board. Knead until smooth. Return to buttered bowl, turn to coat, cover, and let rise until doubled. Punch down, form into two equal loaves, and roll each in corn meal. Place loaves in buttered 7x4-inch pans, cover, and let rise again until doubled. Bake at 400°F. for 25-30 minutes. Makes two 7-inch loaves.

⚜ SALLY LUNN YEAST BREAD ⚜

To avoid doughy fingers, make this ancient and justly famous bread with an electric mixer. Bake in a bundt pan for a very pretty breakfast bread.

3½-4 cups flour	½ cup milk
⅓ cup sugar	½ cup water
1 teaspoon salt	¼ pound butter
1 package dry yeast	3 eggs

In large bowl, mix 1¼ cups flour, sugar, salt, and yeast. Combine milk, water, and butter in saucepan. Heat until warm (butter doesn't need to melt). Gradually add to dry ingredients; beat 2 minutes in mixer. Add eggs and 1 cup flour; beat 2 minutes more. Stir in more flour, enough to make stiff dough. Let rise in covered bowl until doubled. Stir down; beat well (by hand) ½ minute. Place in well-greased, 9-inch tube pan. Let rise again, until doubled. Bake at 325°F. for 45-50 minutes. Makes one 9-inch ring.

⚜ SHREDDED WHEAT BREAD ⚜

A close-textured bread rather like rye bread, but far easier to make.

2 cups boiling water	1 tablespoon brown sugar
2 large shredded wheat biscuits, crushed	1 tablespoon butter
½ cup molasses	1 package dry yeast
1 teaspoon salt	½ cup warm water
	5-6 cups unbleached white flour

In large bowl, pour boiling water over shredded wheat. Add molasses, salt, sugar, and butter. When cooled, add yeast dissolved in warm water, and flour. Turn out onto floured board and knead in last of flour. Return to greased bowl, turn to coat all sides, cover, and let rise until doubled. Punch down and form into two loaves; place in two buttered 7x4-inch loaf pans. Cover with towel, and let rise again until doubled. Bake at 400°F. for 15 minutes, then reduce heat to 350°F. for remaining 30 minutes. Makes two 7-inch loaves.

❧ RICH BREAKFAST-DINNER ROLLS ❧

These versatile rolls are marvelous sugar-glazed as sweet breakfast rolls, or served plain as soft dinner rolls. They freeze well either way. For both plain and glazed rolls, accompanying instructions should advise reheating in a 250°F. oven for 10 minutes.

ROLLS

1½ cups warm milk
1 cup sugar
2 yeast cakes
6-7 cups flour

4 eggs, beaten until light
½ teaspoon salt
½ pound butter, melted

GLAZE

1½ cups confectioners' sugar
2 tablespoons milk

1 teaspoon vanilla

In large bowl, pour warm milk over sugar; add yeast (making sure milk is warm, not hot to touch — about 110°F.). Stir in 3 cups of flour, cover, and let rise 1 hour until bubbly. Then add beaten eggs, salt, butter, and remaining flour. Turn out onto floured board, and knead 5 minutes. (At this point dough may be refrigerated for up to 4 days.) Divide dough into twenty-four balls; place on two buttered cookie sheets — a dozen balls for each. Balls of dough should just touch. Cover with towels, and let rise again until doubled. Bake at 375°F. for 20-30 minutes. To glaze: combine confectioners' sugar, milk, and vanilla, and beat well. Frost baked rolls when they have cooled. Makes 24 rolls.

❧ PAM'S MOTHER'S COFFEE ROLLS ❧

Sour cream gives these dinner rolls special tenderness. They go very well with any of the soups, chowders, or casseroles in Chapter 1.

2 eggs	1 yeast cake
¼ cup sugar	¼ cup warm milk
¼ pound butter, melted	3-4 cups flour
¼ cup sour cream	

In mixing bowl, beat together eggs, sugar, melted butter, and sour cream. Add yeast dissolved in warm milk. Mix in flour until batter is no longer sticky, and you can mold it in your hands. Refrigerate overnight. Next morning, punch down and knead. Form into miniature loaves (3x2-inch) and place on a greased cookie sheet, or roll out on floured board and cut round shapes for rolls. Let rise in warm place 45 minutes, then bake at 375°F. for 10-20 minutes, depending on size. Makes 4-6 miniature loaves, or 12 rolls.

❧ WHEAT STICKS OR ROLLS ❧

These chewy bread sticks make a wonderful appetizer when served with fancy spreads (Chapter 5), or simply with cream cheese and lumpfish caviar. The rolls are good with lunch or dinner.

1 package dry yeast	1 teaspoon salt
1½ cups warm milk	¼ pound butter, melted
1 egg	3 cups whole wheat flour
¼ cup molasses	3 cups unbleached white flour

In large bowl, dissolve yeast in warm milk; stir in egg, molasses, salt, and melted butter. Stir in whole wheat flour, then white flour. Turn out onto floured board and knead, adding more flour if necessary, until dough is smooth and elastic. Return to buttered bowl, turn to coat all sides, cover, and let rise until doubled. Punch down, knead, turn out onto floured board, and roll out ¾ inch thick. Cut in two, and roll each piece into a long loaf. Place on greased cookie sheet, cover, and let rise again until doubled. To make rolls: slice each loaf about two thirds through at 2-inch intervals before baking. Bake at 400°F. for 10-15 minutes. Makes 2 large French sticks or about 20 rolls.

QUICK BREADS AND MUFFINS

APRICOT BREAD

A sweet, fruit-nutty bread. Great plain, or spread with cream cheese. Or toast it and serve with butter.

1 cup dried apricots
warm water to cover
1 cup sugar
2 tablespoons butter, softened
1 egg
1 teaspoon vanilla
¼ cup water
½ cup orange juice
2 cups sifted flour
2 tablespoons baking powder
¼ teaspoon baking soda
¼ teaspoon ground cloves
1 teaspoon salt
½ cup slivered almonds (toasted for 5 minutes at 350°F.)

Soak apricots in warm water for 30 minutes; drain and chop. Set aside. In mixing bowl, cream sugar, butter, egg, and vanilla together. Add water and orange juice. Sift together flour, baking powder, baking soda, cloves, and salt. Stir into creamed mixture. Add apricots. Grind almonds in a blender or chop fine, and stir in. Pour batter into greased 7x4-inch loaf pan, and let sit 20 minutes. Bake at 350°F. for 55-60 minutes. Cool on rack in pan. Makes one 7x4-inch loaf.

BANANA OR PINEAPPLE BREAD

An old standby which can be turned into Apple (use 1 cup apple sauce), or Pear (1 cup crushed pears) Bread.

⅔ cup sugar
4 tablespoons butter, melted
1 egg
1 cup crushed bananas (3 medium bananas), or 1 cup crushed pineapple, drained
2 cups flour
1 teaspoon baking soda
½ teaspoon salt
(½ cup currants)
• • •
apple butter

In mixing bowl, beat together sugar, butter, egg, and fruit. Combine dry ingredients and beat in. Add currants if desired. Pour batter into buttered 7x4-inch loaf pan. Let rest for 20 minutes so the top won't crack when cooked, and bake at 375°F. for 50-60 minutes. Makes one 7-inch loaf.

⚘ CRANBERRY-ORANGE BREAD ⚘

If you have a freezer, make several of these during the cranberry season for a stock of gifts through Thanksgiving and the holiday season. Good either with dinner or as a dessert.

2 cups flour	4 tablespoons butter, melted
1 cup sugar	¾ cup orange juice
1½ teaspoons baking powder	1 egg, beaten
1 teaspoons salt	1 teaspon grated lemon rind
½ teaspoon baking soda	1 cup fresh cranberries, chopped

Sift together dry ingredients; set aside. In mixing bowl with wooden spoon, beat together butter, juice, egg, lemon rind, and cranberries. Stir in dry ingredients until thoroughly mixed. Pour batter into buttered 7x4-inch loaf pan, and bake at 350°F. for 1 hour. Cool loaf in pan 10 minutes before removing to rack. Makes one 7-inch loaf.

⚘ GINGERBREAD ⚘

So moist and tender you can serve it alone, without whipped cream. But send a carton of cream along as an option.

¼ pound butter, softened	½ teaspoon salt
⅔ cup packed light brown sugar	1 teaspoon ginger
1 egg	1 teaspoon cinnamon
½ cup molasses	½ teaspoon ground cloves
½ cup boiling water	• • •
1½ cups flour	*8-ounce carton whipping cream*
1 teaspoon baking soda	

In mixing bowl cream butter with brown sugar and egg. Combine boiling water and molasses in measuring cup and stir. Sift together flour, baking soda, and seasonings in a separate bowl. Gradually add dry ingredients to creamed mixture, alternately with molasses. Pour into buttered 9-inch square pan, and bake at 350°F. for 30 minutes. Serves 9.

LEMON BREAD

A popular offering for church socials, and a superb tea bread as well.

- juice and grated rind of 1 lemon
- 1 cup sugar
- 6 tablespoons butter, melted
- 2 eggs, beaten
- 1½ cups flour
- 1 teaspoon baking powder
- ½ teaspoon salt
- ½ cup sour cream

Add ⅓ cup sugar to lemon juice and set aside. Cream butter and sugar; add eggs and lemon rind. Sift together dry ingredients, and add to the creamed mixture alternately with sour cream. Pour batter into buttered 7x4-inch loaf pan, and bake at 350°F. for 1 hour. Let cool in pan 10 minutes, then pour lemon-sugar mixture over top. Let sit for 1-2 minutes more before removing from pan. Cool on rack. Makes one 7-inch loaf.

MAPLE NUT BREAD

A maple-spicy variation of the standard nut bread.

- 2 cups flour
- 1 teaspoon baking powder
- ½ teaspoon baking soda
- ½ teaspoon salt
- 1 teaspoon cinnamon
- 4 tablespoons butter, melted
- ½ cup packed brown sugar
- 1 egg
- 1 cup *real* maple syrup
- 1 cup finely chopped walnuts

Sift together flour, baking powder, baking soda, salt, and cinnamon; set aside. In mixing bowl, cream together butter, sugar, egg, and maple syrup. Stir in dry ingredients; when well-mixed, add nuts. Pour batter into greased 7x4-inch loaf pan, and bake at 350°F. for 1 hour. Makes one 7-inch loaf.

☙ PAM BURMAN'S SOUR CREAM COFFEE CAKE ☙

My college roommate's mother used to mail this coffee cake to her, and she would divvy out one thin slice to each of us every morning until it was gone. I would spend the rest of my morning classes yearning for another slice.

CAKE

¼ pound butter, melted
½ cup sugar
2 eggs
1 teaspoon vanilla
1½ cups flour

1½ teaspoons baking powder
½ teaspoon baking soda
½ teaspoon salt
½ cup sour cream

STREUSEL

4 tablespoons sugar
4 tablespoons butter, melted
6 tablespoons flour

1 teaspoon cinnamon
½ cup chopped walnuts

Cream butter with sugar; add eggs and vanilla. Sift together dry ingredients. Mix with creamed mixture, about one third at a time, alternating with sour cream. Combine ingredients for streusel in separate bowl. Pour half the cake batter into buttered 7x4-inch loaf pan, and top with half the streusel mixture. Pour in remaining batter, and sprinkle other half of the streusel mixture and walnuts over top. Bake at 350°F. for 35 minutes. Makes one 7-inch loaf.

☙ NUT BREAD ☙

This bread is from my maternal grandmother, Isabel Girling, who used to spread it with Roquefort cheese for little tea sandwiches.

1 egg
½ cup sugar
1 cup milk
1 cup chopped walnuts

2½ cups flour
2½ teaspoons baking powder
¾ teaspoon salt

In mixing bowl, beat egg with sugar; add milk. Combine nuts with dry ingredients and add. Pour into buttered 7x4-inch loaf pan, and let rise 20 minutes. Bake at 300°F. for 50-60 minutes. Makes one 7-inch loaf.

✕ PEAR-CHEESE BREAD ✕

An unusually rich and luscious dessert or tea bread.

4 ounces cream cheese, softened
1 tablespoon vegetable oil
1 cup sugar
2 eggs
1 cup peeled, cored, chopped pears (well-drained canned pears may be substituted)
1 teaspoon freshly grated lemon rind

1 cup flour
2 teaspoons baking powder
½ teaspoon salt
3 tablespoons pear juice, if using canned pears, or apple juice
1 tablespoon fresh lemon juice

In mixing bowl, beat together cream cheese, vegetable oil, and all but 2 tablespoons sugar (reserve for glaze). Beat in eggs until mixture is smooth and fluffy; beat in chopped pears and lemon rind. Sift together flour, baking powder, and salt, and combine with pear mixture. Pour into buttered 7x4-inch loaf pan and bake at 350°F. for 1 hour. To prepare glaze: in a small saucepan mix 2 tablespoons sugar with pear juice and lemon juice, and cook over low heat until sugar has dissolved. When bread is baked, pour glaze over top while in pan. Let rest for 5 minutes, then remove from pan and cool on rack. Makes one 7-inch loaf.

✕ PUMPKIN BREAD ✕

A moist, spicy bread which makes a nice accompaniment with gift soups or chowders, or stands on its own as a tea bread.

3⅓ cups flour
1½ teaspoons salt
1 teaspoon nutmeg
1 teaspoon cinnamon
2 teaspoons baking soda
3 cups sugar

1 cup vegetable oil
⅔ cup water
16-ounce can pumpkin
4 eggs
1½ cups chopped walnuts

Sift dry ingredients into large mixing bowl, add remaining ingredients, and beat until smooth. Divide into three buttered 7x4-inch loaf pans, rest 20 minutes, and bake at 350°F. for 1 hour. Makes three 7-inch loaves.

⚜ *STRAWBERRY-NUT BREAD* ⚜

A delectable dessert bread which makes a timely summer gift, though substituting frozen (unsweetened) strawberries for fresh makes it a possibility for all seasons.

½ cup butter, melted
¾ cup sugar
1 teaspoon vanilla
1 egg
1 cup undrained, crushed
 strawberries

2 cups flour
2 teaspoons baking powder
½ teaspoon baking soda
½ teaspoon salt
½ cup sour cream
⅔ cup finely chopped walnuts

In mixing bowl, beat together butter, sugar, vanila, and egg until fluffy. Add strawberries. Sift dry ingredients together and add to strawberry mixture, alternating with sour cream. Stir in nuts. Pour into buttered 7x4-inch loaf pan and bake at 350°F. for 60-65 minutes. Let cool 10 minutes on wire rack before removing from pan. Makes one 7-inch loaf.

⚜ *SCONES* ⚜

Just right for those who pin their kilts with grouse-foot brooches. Send along some sweet butter and a jar of homemade jam. Reheat in a dampened paper bag in 300°F. oven.

1½ cups flour
1½ tablespoons sugar
¾ teaspoon baking powder
¼ teaspoon baking soda
pinch salt

4 tablespoons butter
7-8 tablespoons buttermilk
• • •
sweet butter
homemade jam

Sift dry ingredients into mixing bowl. Cut in butter with pastry blender until pieces are very fine. Sprinkle with 7 tablespoons buttermilk, and mix with fork until entirely moistened. Add more buttermilk if necessary, and continue stirring until dough forms a ball. Turn dough onto floured surface, knead a few times, and form into two balls. Working with one ball of dough at a time, pat or roll with rolling pin into circle ½ inch thick. Cut each circle into six wedges. Place wedges on cookie sheet and bake at 400°F. for 10 to 12 minutes, or until scones are lightly browned. Makes 12 scones.

❧ APPLE-CINNAMON MUFFINS ❧

Great warm or cold for breakfast or brunch, and terrific served with a pork or ham dinner.

MUFFINS

2¼ cups flour	1 cup milk
3½ teaspoons baking powder	1 egg, beaten
½ teaspoon salt	1 tablespoon butter, melted
½ cup sugar	2 large, or 3 small apples,
1 teaspoon cinnamon	peeled, cored, and chopped

TOPPING

3 tablespoons brown sugar	¼ teaspoon nutmeg

For muffins, sift together dry ingredients, then stir in other muffin ingredients. Fill twelve paper-lined muffin tins two-thirds full. Combine topping ingredients and sprinkle over each. Bake at 400°F. for 15-20 minutes. Make 12 muffins.

❧ BARBARA ZUBE'S BRAN HEALTH MUFFINS ❧

The recipe for these muffins came from a friend in Sarasota, Florida. They are as rich and flavorful as they are nutritious.

1 cup whole bran cereal	¼ cup packed brown sugar
1 cup flour	1 egg, beaten
2 tablespoons wheat germ	¾ cup buttermilk
2 tablespoons toasted sunflower	¼ cup cooking oil
seeds	2 tablespoons honey
1 teaspoon baking soda	(½ cup raisins)

In mixing bowl, stir together bran cereal, flour, wheat germ, sunflower seeds, baking soda, and brown sugar. In separate bowl, combine egg, buttermilk, oil, and honey; mix well into dry ingredients. Add optional raisins. Fill eighteen paper-lined muffin tins two-thirds full. Bake at 400°F. for 15 minutes. Makes 18 muffins.

❦ *CORN MUFFINS* ❦

Plain, these corn muffins are a perfect accompaniment for any soup or meal. With fruit, they're great for breakfast. If you can find stone-ground corn meal, use it; the muffins will taste as though they were made with fresh corn!

1 cup corn meal
1 cup flour
¾ teaspoon salt
2½ teaspoons baking powder
¼ cup sugar

1 cup half and half
2 eggs, beaten
3 tablespoons butter, melted
(1 cup blueberries, blackberries, or cranberries)

In mixing bowl sift dry ingredients. Combine half and half, eggs, and butter, and stir into dry mixture. Add optional berries if desired. Fill twelve paper-lined muffin tins two-thirds full, and bake at 400°F. for 20 minutes. Makes 12 muffins.

❦ *ANN MORRIS'S PEANUT BUTTER MUFFINS* ❦

The rich, peanutty flavor of these muffins is a fine complement to soup. Sliced in half, buttered, and placed under broiler for a minute, they make a great breakfast roll.

1½ cups flour
½ teaspoon salt
4 teaspoons baking powder
1 egg, beaten

½ cup sugar
1 cup milk
½ cup peanut butter

In mixing bowl, sift together flour, salt, and baking powder. In separate bowl, mix egg, sugar, milk, and peanut butter; combine with dry ingredients. Fill twelve paper-lined muffin tins two-thirds full, and bake at 350°F. for 15-20 minutes. Makes 12 muffins.

☙ CHAPTER 3 ☙
Cakes and Pies,
Candy and Snacks

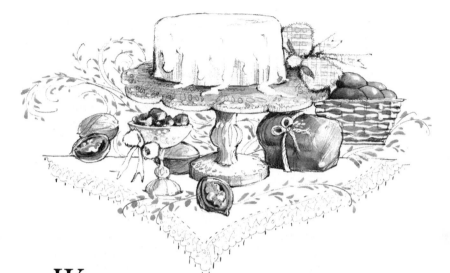

W̲ho doesn't love to receive something sweet as a present, for whatever reason? Especially when one is far from home, a favorite cake or candy received in the mail evokes that warming sense of being loved and thought about even more strongly than a phone call or letter. All of the cakes, candy, and snacks in this chapter* are easily mailed, though of course, they may be wrapped up and given by hand just as well.

Pies are not mailable — indeed even delivering them in person requires careful handling. The traditional New England pie basket, which can be bought to carry either one or two pies, is invaluable. If you don't have a pie basket, fill a shallow box with styrofoam packing material or popcorn, and nestle the pie pan firmly into the packing. Place the box as levelly as possible on the car floor and drive conservatively. The easiest solution is to commandeer a passenger who will undertake to hold the pie level around curves and over bumpy roads.

* *Except the almond layer cake.*

PACKAGING CAKES AND PIES, CANDY AND SNACKS

For cakes and cupcakes, see the packaging instructions for Yeast Breads and Rolls, Quick Breads and Muffins (page 38).

Extra protection is necessary when mailing candy. Layers should be separated by two sheets of waxed paper with two paper towels in between, for brittle candy. Wrap individual pieces of candy in waxed paper before putting in can or box. Coffee cans, decorated as you wish, make excellent candy containers. Any remaining space in the box or coffee can should be filled with paper towels, tissue paper, or plastic bubble wrap.

Seal corrugated mailing box with pressure-sensitive tape, and send package first class, or by UPS whenever possible, to assure freshness. An exception is the Old-Fashioned Fruitcake, which can be mailed by parcel post; sitting in a postal warehouse will only improve its flavor!

For gift pies, I use disposable heavy-duty foil pie pans (be careful to support the bottoms when carrying the pies — foil pans held by the edges as one would a glass pie pan, have a regrettable tendency to buckle, with predictable results). Pies donated to a neighbor or a town or church function can be delivered in your own pie pans; just remember to pick them up!

Instructions for reheating and serving should be written out on a card, or bright square of colored construction paper (verbal instructions are apt to be forgotten), along with other pertinent information, e.g., whether item has already been frozen, whether it may be frozen, etc. Punch a hole in the instructions card and attach it with ribbon, or affix solidly with tape, so it won't become lost.

CAKES

🥄 ALMOND LAYER CAKE WITH EGG YOLK ICING 🥄

A family recipe of Spanish origin, it is somewhat demanding, but is a festive and sumptuous addition to any occasion. You can save the egg whites for meringues. Do not *attempt to mail this cake.*

CAKE

1¾ cups whole blanched
   almonds
2¼ cups sifted cake flour
1½ cups sugar
3½ teaspoons baking powder

1 teaspoon salt
¼ pound butter, softened
1 cup milk
1 teaspoon almond extract
4 egg whites, *un*beaten

FROSTING

1¼ cups sugar
⅓ cup cold water

10 egg yolks

Place almonds on cookie sheet and toast in middle of oven at 325°F. for 10 minutes, shaking occasionally to avoid scorching. Set ½ cup toasted almonds aside; grind the remainder in blender or food processor. Set aside. In mixing bowl, sift together flour, sugar, baking powder, and salt. Beat in butter, ⅔ cup milk, and almond extract for 2 minutes. Add rest of milk, egg whites, and ground almonds; beat 2 minutes more. Grease and flour two 8- or 9-inch round cake pans, and divide batter equally between them. Bake at 350°F. for 30-35 minutes. Cool 10 minutes, then remove from pans.

Prepare frosting. Combine sugar and water in saucepan; cook over medium heat until sugar is dissolved. When syrup begins to simmer and becomes translucent, remove from heat, and let stand until cool to the touch. Meanwhile, place egg yolks in large, heavy saucepan, and beat until thick and light yellow. Beating constantly, dribble in sugar syrup. Place pan over very low heat, and simmer, stirring constantly with a wooden spoon, 10 minutes, or until mixture is smooth and thick enough to coat spoon. Let cool to room temperature. (Frosting will continue to thicken as it cools.) Frost cake, and place reserved whole almonds around the top of the cake. Makes one 2-layer cake.

✄ CHARLOTTE'S
APPLESAUCE CAKE ✄

Delicious either plain or with lemon glaze. If you plan to mail it, leave the cake unglazed, and enclose glaze recipe on accompanying card.

CAKE

1 cup applesauce
¾ cup sugar
1 egg
4 tablespoons butter, melted
2 cups flour
2 teaspoons baking powder

½ teaspoon baking soda
½ teaspoon salt
1 teaspoon cinnamon
¼ teaspoon ground cloves
¼ teaspoon nutmeg
(1 cup chopped raisins)

LEMON GLAZE

1 cup sifted confectioners' sugar
1 teaspoon lemon juice

½ teaspoon grated lemon rind
2 tablespoons milk

In mixing bowl, combine applesauce, sugar, egg, and melted butter. Sift together dry ingredients, and beat into applesauce mixture. Stir in chopped raisins if desired. Pour batter into buttered 11x7-inch pan, and bake at 350°F. for 25-30 minutes. Remove from pan and cool on rack. Mix ingredients of lemon glaze and pour over cake when cool. Serves 8.

✠ APPLE-CIDER CAKE ✠

A fine-textured apple cake, best served warm with softened butter.

2 cups flour	2 eggs
1 teaspoon baking powder	½ cup sweet cider
¼ teaspoon salt	2 apples, peeled, cored, and
¼ pound butter, melted	sliced
½ cup sugar	confectioners' sugar

In small bowl, sift together flour, baking powder, and salt. In large bowl, cream butter and sugar until light and fluffy; add eggs and beat well. Gradually stir in flour and cider alternately. Beat with electric mixer 2 minutes. Butter 8-inch round cake pan and line with circle of buttered waxed paper. Lay rings of sliced apples (each concentric circle in opposite directions) on waxed paper. Pour in batter, and bake at 325°F. for 35 minutes. Let cool 10 minutes before removing from pan; peel off waxed paper. Dust top of cake with confectioners' sugar. Makes one 8-inch layer.

✠ CHOCOLATE ICE-BOX CAKE ✠

A super summer dessert. For gift purposes enclose a half-pint carton of cream and confectioners' sugar in a sandwich bag, or a container of ready-whipped cream. Instructions should read, "Cover top of cake with sweetened whipped cream."

8 ounces semisweet chocolate bits	⅛ teaspoon cream of tartar
3 tablespoons water	18-24 ladyfingers
2 tablespoons sugar	• • •
4 eggs, separated	*1 cup whipping cream*
	1 tablespoon confectioners' sugar

Melt chocolate with water and sugar over very low heat. Add beaten egg yolks, and cook 2 minutes; remove from heat and set aside. Beat egg whites with cream of tartar until stiff, and fold into chocolate mixture. Cut ladyfingers in half lengthwise, and layer in bottom of serving bowl or 13x15-inch pan. Cover with half the chocolate mixture, add a second layer of ladyfingers, and top with remaining chocolate mixture. Chill until set; whip cream with confectioners' sugar, and spread over top. Serves 8.

❧ MELLO'S LAZY DAISY CAKE ❧

A sweet cake for dessert or teas; best delivered by hand.

CAKE

2 eggs	½ teaspoon salt
1 cup sugar	1 tablespoon butter
1 cup flour	½ cup milk
1 teaspoon baking powder	1 teaspoon vanilla

ICING

3 tablespoons butter	2 tablespoons milk
5 tablespoons sugar	½ cup grated coconut

In mixing bowl, beat eggs well, then beat in sugar, then flour sifted with baking powder and salt. Melt butter in milk, and vanilla, and stir. Pour into buttered 8-inch square pan, and bake at 375°F. for 25 minutes. Remove from pan and cool.

Mix icing ingredients in double boiler top over boiling water. Cook for 3-4 minutes. Spread on cooled cake, and brown under broiler briefly. Cut into squares. Serves 10-12.

❧ DUNDEE TEA CAKE BARS ❧

A festive tea cake for fancy occasions.

CAKE

¼ pound butter, softened	1 teaspoon baking powder
½ cup sugar	¼ teaspoon salt
1 teaspoon vanilla	½ teaspoon nutmeg
2 eggs	¾ cup mixed candied fruit
1½ cups flour	¼ cup raisins

LEMON GLAZE

¼ cup sifted confectioners' sugar	½ teaspoon lemon juice
1 teaspoon milk	

In mixing bowl, cream butter and sugar until light. Beat in vanilla and eggs. Sift dry ingredients together, and beat in; stir in fruit and mix well. Butter 9-inch square pan, and line bottom with buttered wax paper. Pour batter into pan, and bake at 325°F. for 25-30 minutes. Turn out on rack and peel off paper. Turn right side up, and brush top with glaze. Cool and cut into bars. Makes 24 bars.

❧ *WINNIE'S CHOCOLATE CAKE* ❧

A super-moist chocolate cake that melts in your mouth. This recipe is not suitable for cupcakes.

CAKE

1 cup sifted flour	2 squares unsweetened chocolate
1 cup sugar	2 tablespoons butter
1 teaspoon baking soda	1 cup milk
1 teaspoon baking powder	1 egg
¼ teaspoon salt	

EMERGENCY FROSTING

1 egg white	3 tablespoons cold water
⅞ cup sugar	½ teaspoon vanilla

Sift dry ingredients together. Melt chocolate and butter in double boiler over boiling water. Stir milk, egg, and chocolate mixture into dry ingredients. Pour into buttered 8x8-inch pan, and bake at 350°F. for 30 minutes. Meanwhile, make frosting. Combine egg white, sugar, and water in double boiler top, and beat 5 minutes over boiling water. Remove from heat, add vanilla, and beat until thick enough to spread. When cake is done, remove from pan and cool on rack. Frost when cool. Cut into squares. Serves 8-10.

✠ OLD-FASHIONED FRUITCAKES ✠

The tour de force *of baked Christmas gifts. Make this recipe at least two weeks ahead, to give the fruitcakes time to age properly.*

1 cup vegetable oil	1 teaspoon ginger
1¼ cups sugar	1 cup brandy
4 eggs	1 cup raisins
¼ cup molasses	1 cup currants
3 cups flour	2 cups chopped dates
1 teaspoon baking powder	1 cup chopped dried apricots
2 teaspoons salt	2 cups mixed candied fruit
2 teaspoons cinnamon	1 cup walnuts
1 teaspoon nutmeg	additional brandy

In large mixing bowl, combine oil, sugar, eggs, and molasses. Beat with electric mixer for 2 minutes. Sift 2 cups flour, baking powder, salt, and spices together; stir into oil mixture alternately with brandy. Add remaining 1 cup flour to fruits and nuts, and combine with batter, mixing thoroughly. Butter two 9x5-inch loaf pans, and line with buttered, heavy brown wrapping paper. Pour batter into pans and bake at 275°F. for 2½ hours. Cool 15 minutes before removing from pans. Cool thoroughly on rack before peeling off paper. Wrap in aluminum foil, and let age in a cool place for at least 2 weeks, sprinkling brandy on the tops daily. Makes two 9x5-inch loaves.

PIES

What really makes or breaks a pie is, of course, the pastry. The most elegant filling is worthless if enclosed in a leathery crust. Making a foolproof, light, flaky pastry from scratch can be a life-time study.

The two pastry crust recipes below are almost foolproof. Without accounting for extra-dry air, low-pressure systems, or the relative positions of the planets, these will work 98% of the time. The graham cracker crust never fails, and of course, there are excellent frozen pie crusts on the market today.

All recipes use 9- or 10-inch pie pans interchangeably.

❧ PLAIN PASTRY ❧

2 cups flour
1 teaspoon salt
¾ cup vegetable shortening
3-4 tablespoons cold water

In medium mixing bowl, sift flour with salt. Cut in shortening with pastry blender or two knives until pieces are pea-size. Sprinkle cold water over mixture (I use an old-fashioned laundry sprinkler), and stir with fork until mixture holds together. Divide in half, and roll out to desired thickness on floured pastry cloth. Makes pastry for 2-crust pie in 9- or 10-inch pie pan.

❧ FANCY PASTRY ❧

This recipe may be doubled for a two-crust pie.

1½ cups flour
1½ teaspoons sugar
½ teaspoon salt
4 tablespoons cold butter, cut into pieces
4 tablespoons vegetable shortening
3 tablespoons cold water

In mixing bowl, sift flour, sugar, and salt. Cut in butter and vegetable shortening with pastry blender or two knives until pieces are pea-size. Sprinkle with cold water, and mix together with fork until dough comes together. Form into a ball. (At this point dough may be wrapped in plastic wrap and refrigerated.) If you wish to use right away, roll out on floured pastry cloth. For a pre-baked pie shell, flute edges if necessary, prick bottom and sides of pie crust with fork, and bake at 450°F. for 10 minutes, or until light golden in color. For an unbaked pie shell, flute and prick as above, and pour in filling. Makes 1 pie shell.

❧ GRAHAM CRACKER CRUST ❧

1½ cups graham cracker crumbs (18 single crackers)

3 tablespoons sugar
⅓ cup butter, melted

Combine all ingredients, and mix thoroughly. Press crumbs against bottom and sides of pie plate (by pressing a pie plate of the same size inside the first pie plate on top of the crumbs). Bake at 350°F. for 10 minutes. Cool. Makes 1 pie shell.

❧ SARAH'S APPLE PIE ❧

This is my daughter Sarah's favorite pie, even uncooked. She used to steal the cinnamon-sugared apple slices and scraps of raw dough as I was making it. A block of Cheddar cheese makes a nice accompaniment.

10 large McIntosh apples, peeled, cored, and sliced
1 cup sugar
1½ teaspoon cinnamon

fancy pastry, (page 65), doubled
• • •
Cheddar cheese

In large bowl, mix apple slices with sugar and cinnamon; set aside. Mix pastry, divide in half, and roll out bottom crust. Lay in 10-inch pie pan, fill with apples, dampen crust around rim with water to seal, and roll out top crust. Lay crust over apples, trim both crusts to 1 inch over rim, tuck under, and flute. Slash top crusts to vent, and bake at 425°F. for 50 minutes. Yields 6 huge slices, or 8 polite slices.

❧ RUSTY'S APPLE PIE ❧

A variation on traditional recipes, this apple pie's rich and delicious flavor will win you friends. Tastes good, warm or cold.

10 large McIntosh apples, peeled, cored, and sliced
plain pastry (page 65)
1 cup sugar
2 tablespoons flour
⅓ pound Cheddar cheese, cut in ¾-inch cubes
3 tablespoons butter, melted
¼ cup molasses

Prepare apples, and set aside. Make pastry, roll out bottom crust, and line 10-inch pie pan. Mix sugar with flour, and sprinkle 3 tablespoons of this mixture over bottom pie crust. Next add half the sliced apples, a layer of cheese chunks, half the remaining sugar/flour mixture, and remaining apples. Dot with melted butter, add remaining sugar/flour mixture, and pour molasses over all. Dampen pie crust around rim. Roll out top crust, and place over all. Trim both crusts to 1 inch over rim, tuck under, and flute edge. Cut vents in top crust, and bake at 400°F. for 50-60 minutes. Serves 6-8.

⚜ CHOCOLATE ANGEL PIE ⚜

Meringue, chocolate, whipped cream, and nuts — need I say more? Dinner-party fare. Must be served cold.

2 egg whites
⅛ teaspoon salt
⅛ teaspoon cream of tartar
½ cup granulated sugar
½ cup finely chopped nuts
½ teaspoon vanilla

6 ounces semisweet chocolate bits
2 tablespoons water
1 tablespoon coffee liqueur
1 cup whipping cream, whipped
shaved unsweetened baker's chocolate

Beat egg whites with salt and cream of tartar until foamy. Add sugar gradually, beating until very stiff peaks hold. Fold in nuts and vanilla. Spread in buttered 9-inch pie pan, building mixture up one-half inch above sides of pan. Bake at 300°F. for 50-55 minutes. Cool.

Melt chocolate bits in water over low heat, stirring constantly. When melted, stir in liqueur. Remove from heat and cool slightly, then fold into whipped cream. Pile into meringue shell, and refrigerate at least 2 hours. When set, sprinkle shaved chocolate over top. Serves 6-8.

⚜ LEMON CHIFFON PIE ⚜

Enclose a carton of whipping cream. Instructions: serve pie cold, topped with a thin layer of whipped cream.

fancy pastry
4 eggs, separated
1 cup sugar
juice of 1½ lemons
3 tablespoons grated lemon rind

1½ teaspoons unflavored gelatin
3 tablespoons cold water

• • •

½ pint whipping cream

Make and bake pastry shell according to directions on page 65. Meanwhile, in double boiler top, beat egg yolks, then beat in ½ cup sugar, lemon juice, and lemon rind. Cook over boiling water until thick. Add gelatin softened in 1 tablespoon water. Remove double-boiler top and allow to cool slightly. In separate bowl, beat egg whites until stiff; then beat in remaining cold water and ½ cup sugar. Fold egg whites into cooked mixture. Pile into pie shell, and chill. Makes one 9- or 10-inch pie.

❦ GRASSHOPPER PIE ❦

This rich, minty pie would be a welcome contribution to a neighborhood dinner party. Must be kept refrigerated and served cold.

24 plain chocolate wafer cookies (enough to make 1½ cups crumbs)
⅔ cup sugar
¼ cup butter, melted
1 envelope unflavored gelatin
½ cup water
¼ teaspoon salt
3 egg yolks

¼ cup crème de menthe
¼ cup coffee liqueur
(green food coloring)
ice and cold water
4 egg whites
⅛ teaspoon cream of tartar
1 cup whipping cream
semisweet chocolate shavings

Crush chocolate wafers. Combine with 1 teaspoon sugar and melted butter. Press into 9-inch pie plate and bake 12 minutes at 375°F. Meanwhile, soften gelatin in water in saucepan. Add ⅓ cup sugar, ⅛ teaspoon salt, and egg yolks. Cook over low heat, stirring constantly until gelatin has dissolved and mixture has thickened; do not allow to boil. Remove from heat and add liqueurs. Add optional food coloring. Fill a bowl with ice and cold water, immerse bottom of saucepan, and stir mixture constantly until cool and the consistency of an unbeaten egg white (about 5 minutes). Remove from ice water.

Beat egg whites with cream of tartar and remaining salt into soft peaks. Gradually beat in remaining sugar to stiff peaks, then fold into liqueur mixture. Spoon filling into chocolate-crumb crust, and sprinkle generously with chocolate shavings. Chill for at least 2 hours. Serves 6-8.

✖ MINCEMEAT ICE CREAM PIE ✖

If you eat Thanksgiving or Christmas dinner with neighbors, and contribute to the feast — here is a great way to do so. Bring along the extra mincemeat in a small jar, and the ice cream in its carton. Advise that pie should be served warm, with ice cream layered over top. The extra mincemeat is to be heated and spooned over the ice cream.

plain pastry (page 65)
28- to 30-ounce jar mincemeat
¼ cup dark rum or brandy

• • •

1 cup mincemeat
1-quart carton vanilla ice cream

Prepare pastry. Roll out bottom crust and line 10-inch pie pan. Mix mincemeat with rum or brandy, and pour all but 1 cup into pastry-lined 10-inch pie plate. Dampen rim of bottom crust, cover with top crust, trim, seal, and press edges with fork. (I prefer a fork-sealed edge to fluting for mincemeat pies, for no known reason.) Cut small center vents, and bake at 425°F. for 35 minutes. Cover pie with ice cream and spoon extra mincemeat mixture over top. Serves 8.

✖ ORANGE-RHUBARB PIE ✖

A tangy, citrus-flavored rhubarb pie, good served either warm or cold. Use less sugar for early rhubarb, which is not as tart.

1½ to 1¾ cups sugar
⅓ cup flour
4 cups cut-up rhubarb
2 oranges, peeled, sectioned, and diced

1 teaspoon grated orange peel
plain pastry (page 65)
1½ tablespoons butter, melted
sugar

In a large bowl, mix together sugar and flour; stir in rhubarb, oranges, and orange peel. Pour into 9- or 10-inch pastry-lined pie pan, dot with melted butter, and dampen edges of crust around rim to help seal. Cover with top crust, trim, seal, and flute. Slash vents in top crust, sprinkle with sugar, and bake at 425°F. for 40-50 minutes. Serves 8.

✄ PEACH PIE ✄

A creamy-textured pie at its best made with fresh peaches. Accompanying instructions should advise that the pie should be served warm, each piece à la mode with a dollop of the ice cream sent along in its carton.

PIE

graham cracker crust (page 66)
4 cups peeled, pitted, and
   quartered peaches
½ cup sugar

½ teaspoon cinnamon
1 egg
2 tablespoons whipping cream

TOPPING

¼ cup packed brown sugar
½ cup flour
¼ cup butter, melted

• • •

vanilla ice cream

Make graham cracker crust in 9-inch pie plate and bake according to instructions. Meanwhile, in large bowl, mix peaches with combined sugar and cinnamon. Beat together egg and cream and add to peaches; pour into cooled graham cracker crust. Combine topping ingredients and sprinkle over top. Bake at 425°F. for 35 minutes. Serves 6-8.

✄ PUMPKIN PIE ✄

There's a deep satisfaction in growing and cooking your own pumpkins for this traditional autumn pie, but if you don't go the whole route, canned pumpkin is really every bit as good.

fancy pastry (page 65)
2 cups mashed cooked or
   canned pumpkin (if cooked
   fresh, make sure to drain well)
¾ teaspoon salt
1½ cups cream
2 eggs

¾ cup packed brown sugar
1 tablespoon butter, melted
1¼ teaspoons cinnamon
¼ teaspoon ginger
¼ teaspoon nutmeg
pinch ground cloves

Make pastry and line 10-inch pie pan. Mix all ingredients and pour into unbaked shell. Bake at 425°F. for 45 minutes, or until center of pie has set. Serves 8.

❧ *STRAWBERRY-CHEESE PIE* ❧

The pie-maker's answer to cheese cake — as rich, light, and delicious as anything made in a spring-form pan. Include a ½-pint carton of sour cream with the pie. Accompanying instructions should advise to serve cold, with sour cream dolloped over top.

graham cracker crust (page 66)
2 eggs, well beaten
⅔ cup sugar
two 8-ounce packages cream
   cheese
1 teaspoon fresh lemon juice
½ teaspoon grated lemon rind

1 teaspoon vanilla
½ teaspoon cinnamon
2 cups hulled, halved
   strawberries
½ cup sugar
• • •
½ pint sour cream

Make graham cracker crust (page 66) and bake. Meanwhile, beat together eggs and sugar. Add cream cheese to egg mixture, beating until smooth. Add lemon juice, rind, vanilla, and cinnamon. Fill crust and bake at 350°F. for 25-30 minutes. Cool. Mix strawberries and sugar, and spread over top of pie. Refrigerate. Serves 6-8.

TARTS

*T*arts may, of course, be filled with anything that fills pies — fruit, pudding, custard, ice cream — but they have the psychological advantage of being a self-contained unit. A person eats only part of a pie, but all of a tart. Here are some easy recipes.

✠ TART PASTRY ✠

Make plain pastry (page 65), and divide into eight equal parts. Roll each part into 4-inch rounds (use a 4-inch diameter bowl, or cardboard template to cut shapes). Place rounds over the backs of custard cups and make four pleats to fit; or line cups of tart or muffin tins with pastry. Shells molded over custard cups must be pre-baked; shells in tart or muffin tins may or may not be baked, according to filling. To pre-bake, prick bottoms with fork, place custard cups or lined tins on cookie sheet, and bake at 475°F. for 8-10 minutes.

✠ STRAWBERRY CHIFFON TARTS ✠

⅔ cup sugar	¼ teaspoon cream of tartar
1 envelope unflavored gelatin	⅓ cup sugar
1 cup hulled crushed	½ cup whipping cream
strawberries	8 whole strawberries, hulled
3 egg whites	tart pastry, prebaked

In saucepan, blend ⅔ cup sugar, gelatin, and strawberries. Bring to full boil, stirring constantly. Place pan in ice water, and stir until mixture has consistency of uncooked egg white. Set aside. Beat egg whites with cream of tartar, gradually adding ⅓ cup sugar, until mixture forms hard peaks. Whip cream separately and fold into meringue. Fold crushed strawberries into mixture, and spoon into pre-baked tart shells. Garnish with whole strawberries. Chill 2 hours, or until set. Makes 8 tarts.

❧ BLUEBERRY TARTS ❧

1 tablespoon fresh lemon juice
6 cups fresh blueberries
1 cup sugar
1 tablespoon flour

½ teaspoon cinnamon
pinch nutmeg
tart pastry (page 73), unbaked

In mixing bowl, sprinkle lemon juice over blueberries. Combine sugar, flour, cinnamon, and nutmeg, and mix with blueberries. Spoon into eight pastry-lined tart pans, place on cookie sheets, and bake at 400°F. for 20 minutes. Makes 8 tarts.

❧ PECAN TARTS ❧

3 eggs
⅔ cup packed brown sugar
½ teaspoon salt
⅓ cup butter, melted

1 cup corn syrup
1 teaspoon vanilla
1 cup pecan halves
tart pastry (page 73), unbaked

Beat eggs, sugar, salt, butter, corn syrup, and vanilla together; mix in pecan halves. Spoon mixture into unbaked tart pastry shells, and bake on cookie sheet at 375°F. for 25-30 minutes. Makes 8 tarts.

CANDY

🌾 DOT MORRIS'S BIRTHDAY CANDY 🌾

These crunchy, toffee-almond flavored pieces should be stored in a tin box, separated by sheets of waxed paper.

½ pound butter
1¼ cups sugar
2 tablespoons water
1 tablespoon light corn syrup

1 teaspoon vanilla
8 ounces semisweet chocolate
2 cups blanched, chopped
  almonds

In heavy saucepan, combine butter, sugar, water, and corn syrup. Cook over low heat until mixture reaches 310°F. on candy thermometer. Remove from heat, and stir in vanilla. Pour out on large, flat, buttered, slightly warmed, cookie sheet, spreading evenly with spatula. Let cool. When toffee has cooled and hardened, warm sheet again in order to melt butter, and gently slide toffee slab off onto a flat surface. Cover top with waxed paper and flip over. In small saucepan melt chocolate over low heat, pour half over top of toffee, and sprinkle with half the chopped almonds. Refrigerate 15 minutes; then turn over and cover with remaining chocolate and almonds. Break into bite-size pieces. Makes ½ pound.

❧ CANDIED FRUIT PEEL ❧

This candy looks very pretty packed in clear glass containers or apothecary jars.

6 large oranges, or 3 large
   grapefruit
water to cover
6-ounce package fruit-flavored
   gelatin

2 cups water
1 stick cinnamon
10 whole cloves
2 cups sugar

Wash oranges or grapefruit. Make cuts in skin and pith from end to end, dividing the skin into four equal sections. Remove peel and white pith in one piece from each section with fingers; reserve fruit for other use. Discard white portion of pith. Cut peel (zest) into one-quarter-inch strips, place in large, heavy enamel or stainless-steel saucepan with water to cover. Boil, covered, for 30 minutes, or until peel can be easily pierced with a fork. Drain. Mix gelatin with 2 cups water and spices, and add to fruit in saucepan. Cover, bring to boil, reduce heat, and simmer for about 50 minutes until syrup is almost absorbed, stirring frequently towards end to prevent sticking. Lift out peel with tongs, and roll in pan sprinkled with sugar until heavily coated. Cool on waxed paper, and store in air-tight containers. Makes about 72 candied peels.

❧ SOUR CREAM FUDGE ❧

A delightful variation for fudge lovers.

2 squares baker's chocolate
⅔ cup sour cream
2 cups sugar

½ teaspoon vanilla
salt

In heavy saucepan, melt chocolate over very low heat. Add sour cream and sugar, and cook to soft-ball stage (230°F.). Remove from heat, add vanilla, and cool. Pour onto marble slab or platter. Sprinkle with a little salt, and work with spatula back and forth until fudge forms ball. Butter the slab or use a cookie sheet and roll out fudge to ½-inch thickness. Let stand until hardened. Cut in squares. Makes ¼ pound of fudge.

❧ CHOCOLATE FUDGE ❧

This is my sister Judy's recipe, and she points out that the same ingredients cooked for a shorter time make a great chocolate sauce.

2 cups sugar	2 tablespoons light corn syrup
⅔ cup milk	2 tablespoons butter
2 squares baker's chocolate	1 teaspoon vanilla
⅛ teaspoon salt	(1 cup chopped nuts)

In medium saucepan, mix sugar, milk, chocolate, salt, and corn syrup. Stir over low heat until chocolate is melted. Increase heat, and boil steadily until mixture reaches the soft-ball stage (236°F.), stirring frequently to prevent burning. Remove from heat and add butter. Set aside to cool (until pan is cool enough to hold bottom in palm of hand). Add vanilla and beat with a spoon until thoroughly mixed and no longer glossy. Pour into buttered 9-inch square pan (top with nuts if desired). When set, cut into squares. Makes 36 pieces.

❧ MAPLE-ALMOND FUDGE ❧

Send this to friends who have moved out of New England to make them homesick. Tell them that this fudge should be stored in an air-tight tin with waxed paper between each layer.

1 cup whole almonds	¼ teaspoon salt
2 cups packed brown sugar	2 tablespoons butter
1 cup maple sugar	1 teaspoon vanilla
1 cup granulated white sugar	½ teaspoon maple flavoring
1 cup heavy cream	

Toast almonds on cookie sheet for 6-7 minutes at 350°F.; watch carefully for scorching. Set aside. In heavy saucepan, combine sugars, cream, and salt. Cook over medium heat, stirring constantly, until sugars dissolve. Boil over medium heat, stirring frequently to prevent sticking, until soft-ball stage (236°F.). Cook 6 minutes longer and remove from heat. Stir in butter; let stand about an hour (until bottom of pan feels just warm to the palm of your hand). Stir in vanilla and maple flavoring, and beat until mixture is creamy. Butter 9-inch square pan, sprinkle almonds in bottom, and spread fudge mixture over nuts. When hardened, cut into 36 pieces.

✣ PENUCHE ✣

The old-fashioned vanilla-flavored, caramel-colored fudge.

3 cups packed brown sugar
1 cup light cream
1 tablespoon butter

1 teaspoon vanilla
1 cup chopped nuts (walnuts or pecans)

In heavy saucepan, cook sugar and cream to soft-ball stage (236°F.). Remove from heat; add butter, vanilla, and nuts, and let cool. Beat until mixture loses its gloss. Turn into greased 9-inch square pan, cool, and cut into squares. Makes 36 pieces.

✣ POPCORN-PEANUT BALLS ✣

A real treat for children, or child-like adults at Christmas time or any time. Wrap each ball in plastic wrap, place several in a clear plastic bag, and tie neck of bag with a ribbon.

7 cups popped popcorn
1 cup unsalted peanuts
1 cup packed light brown sugar
⅓ cup water

⅓ cup light corn syrup
1 teaspoon salt
¼ cup butter
1 teaspoon vanilla

Mix popcorn and peanuts in large bowl; set aside. In heavy saucepan, mix sugar, water, syrup, salt, and butter. Boil over medium-high heat to 250°F. on candy thermometer. Remove from heat and stir in vanilla. Pour slowly over popcorn and peanuts, stirring constantly to mix well. Butter hands, and shape into balls. Makes 8 balls.

SNACKS

Here are recipes for snacks so tasty that no one will mind that they are nutritious. Friends whose hobby is hiking, cross-country skiing, mountaineering, or other strenuous sport will welcome a snack jar.

✙ ALMOND CRUNCH GRANOLA ✙

A sweet, crunchy snack that could double as cocktail fare.

2 cups cornflakes
1 cup slivered almonds
¼ cup maple syrup

⅓ cup vegetable oil
¼ teaspoon salt
½ teaspoon vanilla

Mix all ingredients together, and spread on buttered cookie sheet. Bake at 325°F. for 20-25 minutes. Cool and fill ½-pint jars with screw-on tops. Cover. Makes 3 jars.

✙ SPICED WALNUTS, PECANS, AND ALMONDS ✙

Serve these spiced nuts before or after dinner on holiday occasions. A decorated tin box is the perfect gift container.

2 tablespoons cold water
2 egg whites, lightly beaten
¾ cup packed brown sugar
¼ teaspoon ground cloves
¼ teaspoon salt

½ teaspoon cinnamon
1 cup walnut halves
1 cup pecan halves
1 cup whole blanched almonds

In small bowl, combine water, egg whites, sugar, and seasonings. Beat well. Dip nuts piece by piece into mixture and place on buttered cookie sheet. Bake at 275°F. for 45 minutes, or until golden. Cool and store in covered containers. Makes about 3 cups.

✠ HOPE TAYLOR'S ENERGY CHEWS ✠

A high-protein snack, cookie-like, with a chewy texture.

½ cup butter
1½ cups honey
4 tablespoons cocoa-flavored
  protein powder
1 cup grated apple, cored and
  peeled

¼ teaspoon salt
½ teaspoon cinnamon
3 cups rolled oats
1 cup chopped nuts, or grated
  coconut
1 teaspoon vanilla

In heavy saucepan, combine butter, honey, protein powder, apple, salt, and cinnamon. Boil for 1 minute, stirring constantly; remove from heat. Add oats, nuts or grated coconut, and vanilla; blend well. Arrange cookie-size forkfuls on waxed paper. When hardened, place in covered container, with waxed paper between the layers. Store in refrigerator. Makes about 30.

✠ PEANUT BUTTER GRANOLA ✠

A crunchy, high-energy mix, with an appealing, nutty flavor not unlike fruit cake. Good to take along on a hike or bike trip. Has a shelf life of two weeks; refrigerate if you want to store it longer.

3 cups rolled oats
1 cup salted sunflower seeds
1 cup chopped walnuts
½ cup wheat germ
½ cup packed light brown sugar

4 tablespoons water
¼ cup vegetable oil
½ cup peanut butter
¼ teaspoon vanilla
1 cup raisins

In large bowl, combine oats, sunflower seeds, nuts, and wheat germ; set aside. In small saucepan, heat over medium high heat sugar, water, and oil, and beat with whisk until smooth. Remove from heat, and stir in peanut butter and vanilla. Pour over oats mixture, stirring until evenly coated. Spread mixture over buttered cookie sheet and bake at 250°F. for 40 minutes, stirring every 10 minutes or so. Cool and add raisins. Store in covered ½-pint jars; makes about 8 jars.

❧ CEREAL NIBBLES ❧

A great way to use up cold cereal that has lost its crisp. Sweet snack for kids — too sweet for cocktails.

6 cups unsweetened cold cereal
2 cups dry roasted, unsalted
  peanuts
¼ cup sunflower kernels

½ cup packed brown sugar
¼ cup maple syrup
4 tablespoons butter

    In large bowl, combine cereal, peanuts, and sunflower kernels. Set aside. Stir all other ingredients in small saucepan, and cook over medium heat until sugar is dissolved. Pour over cereal mixture, stirring until evenly covered. Spread mixture on buttered cookie sheet, and bake at 275°F. for 45 minutes, stirring every so often. Cool and store in covered jars. Makes about 8 cups.

✗ *CHAPTER 4* ✗
Cookies, Bars, and Baker's Clay

*A*round our house, cookies are the thing most frequently made for the purpose of giving away, but often
don't make it out of the house. Cookie baking is a project
most children enjoy — especially rolling, cutting, and frosting — and everyone, children and adults too, likes to receive them. Cookies always fill the bill for holiday giving,
and are equally welcome at teas, scout meetings, school occasions, or church functions. (If you work away from home,
bring an occasional gift of cookies to the office — your co-
workers will love you.)

This chapter includes my sister-in-law's special recipe
for pre-colored baker's clay from which Christmas-tree and
other ornaments can be made. These too are kitchen gifts;
though you can't **eat** the ornaments, they can last a life-
time.

PACKAGING COOKIES, BARS, AND BAKER'S CLAY

Colorful plastic plates and plastic wrap are perfect packaging for cookies and squares to be hand-delivered. Or, for cookies, use the cylindrical containers from potato chips. You can bake the squares and bars right in foil pans from the supermarket. Tin boxes cost more, but afford more protection and make a handsomer gift.

See Chapter 3 for mailing instructions; cookies require padding between layers. When mailing Baker's Clay items, be sure there is plenty of filler material in the mailing box as buffer; Barbara uses popcorn.

COOKIES AND BARS

APPLE RAISIN COOKIES

A king-size cookie with a sweet apple-rum flavoring; a perfect gift for friends with big appetites.

½ cup raisins
⅓ cup rum
½ cup honey
4 tablespoons butter
1 egg
2 cups whole wheat flour

½ teaspoon baking soda
¼ teaspoon salt
½ cup chopped walnuts
2 apples, peeled, cored, and chopped

Soak raisins in rum for at least an hour; set aside. In heavy saucepan, heat honey and butter together; when butter is melted, scrape into mixing bowl. Stir in egg, raisins, and rum. Combine flour, baking soda, and salt, and add to honey/butter mixture. Stir in nuts and apples. Use ¼ cup dough for each cookie; drop onto a buttered cookie sheet, 4 inches apart. Bake at 350°F. for 15-20 minutes. Makes 12 *large* cookies.

☙ ITALIAN ALMOND KISSES AND BUTTER BALLS ☙

A friend, Millie Pezzillo, of Cranston, Rhode Island, has built a small business* selling an assortment of homebaked Italian cookies. These are two of the delicious varieties which she includes in her selection.

ITALIAN ALMOND KISSES: *Colorful candy-like drop cookies.*

8 ounces almond paste
1 cup sugar
2 egg whites
¼ cup sifted flour
¼ cup confectioners' sugar

½ cup finely chopped mixed
  candied fruit
½ cup slivered blanched
  almonds

In medium bowl, use fingers to combine almond paste, sugar, and egg whites into smooth paste. Still kneading, work in flour and sugar, then candied fruit. Drop mixture by teaspoons onto a lightly greased cookie sheet, 2 inches apart. Poke a few almond slivers into top of each cookie. Bake at 300°F. for 20-25 minutes. Remove from cookie sheets immediately and cool on wire rack. Makes about 4 dozen.

BUTTER BALLS: *Powdery little balls with a rich, buttery flavor.*

½ pound butter, softened
½ cup confectioners' sugar
1 teaspoon vanilla
2 cups flour

¼ teaspoon salt
1 cup finely chopped pecans
confectioners' sugar

In mixing bowl, cream butter, sugar, and vanilla. Add flour, salt, and nuts; mix well. Shape into 1-inch balls, and bake at 400°F. for 10-12 minutes. While still warm, roll in confectioners' sugar. Makes 5 dozen small cookies.

*Italian Heritage, 53 Westfield Drive, Cranston, RI 02920

⚝ HOPE'S CHEWY BROWNIES ⚝

Just the thing to mail to children away at school or college during exams.

2 squares unsweetened chocolate
¼ pound butter
1 cup sugar
2 eggs, well beaten
1 teaspoon vanilla

⅔ cup flour
½ teaspoon baking powder
¼ teaspoon salt
(½ cup chopped walnuts)

In small saucepan, melt chocolate and butter over low heat. Beat sugar, eggs, and vanilla together in mixing bowl; add chocolate mixture and beat thoroughly. Sift together flour, baking powder, and salt; stir into chocolate mixture. Stir in nuts if desired. Pour into buttered 8-inch square pan, and bake at 350°F. for 25 minutes. Cut into 1x2-inch bars. Makes 32.

⚝ CHOCOLATE CHIP BLOND BROWNIES ⚝

These brownies are like chewy chunks of chocolate chip cookies, another favorite of children in school or college. Unlike chocolate chip cookies, they mail well.

¼ pound butter, melted
1 cup packed brown sugar
1 egg
1 teaspoon vanilla
1 cup sifted flour
½ teaspoon baking powder

⅛ teaspoon baking soda
½ teaspoon salt
(½ cup chopped nuts)
6-ounce package semisweet
  chocolate bits

In mixing bowl, beat together butter, sugar, egg, and vanilla. Sift flour, baking powder, baking soda, and salt; stir into butter/sugar mixture. Add nuts, if desired. Spread in buttered 8-inch square pan and bake at 350°F. for 20-25 minutes. Cool and cut into 2-inch squares. Makes 16.

☙ CHOCOLATE DROPS ☙

A simple and simply mouth-watering chocolate cookie.

¼ pound butter
4 squares unsweetened chocolate
2 cups sugar
4 eggs
2 teaspoons vanilla

2 cups flour
2 teaspoons baking powder
¾ teaspoon salt
granulated sugar

In small saucepan, melt butter and chocolate together over low heat. Scrape into mixing bowl and beat in sugar, eggs, and vanilla. Sift together flour, baking powder, and salt; stir into chocolate mixture. Chill 2 hours. Form walnut-size balls and roll in granulated sugar. Press gently down on buttered cookie sheets, and bake at 350°F. for 12-14 minutes. Makes 6 dozen cookies.

☙ LOIS LUND'S CREAM CHEESE COOKIES ☙

A rich vanilla-flavored cookie.

1 cup butter, softened
8-ounce package cream cheese,
  softened
1 cup sugar

2 cups flour
1 teaspoon salt
3 teaspoons vanilla

In mixing bowl, cream together butter and cheese; add other ingredients and mix well. From a roll 1½ inches in diameter, wrap in waxed paper, and refrigerate for several hours. Slice very thin (I use a wire cheese slicer), and bake at 325°F. for 7-8 minutes. Watch carefully because they burn easily. Makes about 3 dozen cookies.

☙ COCONUT JUMBLES ☙

Moist and delicious cookies for coconut fans.

¼ pound butter, softened
1 cup packed brown sugar
½ cup granulated sugar
2 eggs
1 cup sour cream

1 teaspoon vanilla
2¾ cups sifted flour
½ teaspoon baking soda
1 teaspoon salt
1 cup shredded coconut

In mixing bowl, cream butter with sugars. Beat in eggs. Add sour cream and vanilla. Sift together flour, baking soda, and salt, stir into first mixture. Add coconut and mix well. Drop dough by tablespoons on buttered cookie sheets, 2 inches apart. Bake at 375°F. for 10-12 minutes. Makes about 4 dozen.

✗ CONGO BARS ✗

Bring these when asked to serve refreshments for the local cub or girl scout troop — they'll eat 'em right up!

2¾ cups sifted flour	2½ cups packed brown sugar
2½ teaspoons baking powder	1 teaspoon vanilla
½ teaspoon salt	1 cup chopped nuts
¼ pound plus 2 tablespoons butter, softened	6-ounce package semisweet chocolate chips

Sift together flour, baking powder, and salt; set aside. Beat together butter, sugar, and vanilla. Add dry ingredients, then nuts and chocolate chips. Place in buttered 9x13-inch pan, and bake at 350°F. for 35 minutes. Cool and cut into twenty-four 1x4½-inch rectangles.

✗ HOPE TAYLOR'S CHOCOLATE CHIP COOKIES ✗

Everyone likes chocolate chip cookies — at least everyone I know.

½ pound butter, melted	2 cups flour
1 cup packed brown sugar	1 teaspoon baking soda
¾ cup granulated sugar	1 teaspoon salt
1½ teaspoons vanilla	12-ounce package semisweet chocolate bits
2 eggs	
2 tablespoons water	

In large mixing bowl, beat butter, sugars, vanilla, eggs, and water until creamy. Sift together flour, soda, and salt and add, mixing thoroughly. Add chocolate bits. Drop by teaspoons on buttered cookie sheets, and bake at 375°F. for 7-8 minutes. Makes 6 dozen cookies.

❧ FINNISH SPICE COOKIES ❧

These spicy brown cookies make a flavorful addition to a holiday assortment.

4 tablespoons butter, softened	¼ teaspoon ground cardamom
½ cup packed brown sugar	¼ teaspoon cinnamon
1 egg	⅛ teaspoon ground cloves
1 cup flour	¼ teaspoon salt
1 teaspoon baking powder	¼ cup sour cream

In mixing bowl, cream butter and sugar; add egg and beat until creamy. Combine dry ingredients and beat in, alternating with sour cream. Drop by teaspoons, 2 inches apart, onto buttered cookie sheet, and bake at 375°F. for 8-10 minutes. Makes about 30 cookies.

❧ AUNT HELEN'S FILLED COOKIES ❧

Sugar cookies with a raisin filling. These make a good-sized cookie — two could substitute for lunch. Hint — to speed up creaming butter and sugar, do it in a metal or other heat-proof bowl set on the stove over low heat.

COOKIES

½ cup butter, softened	3½ cups flour
1 cup sugar	3 teaspoons baking powder
1 egg	½ teaspoon salt
1 teaspoon vanilla	½ cup milk

FILLING

1 cup chopped raisins	3 teaspoons flour
¼ cup sugar	½ cup hot water

In mixing bowl, cream butter and sugar. Beat in egg and vanilla. Sift together flour, baking powder, and salt. Stir into butter mixture, alternating with milk. Cover and refrigerate.

To make filling: In heavy saucepan, combine raisins, sugar, flour, and water; stir over medium heat until thickened. Remove from heat.

Roll out dough on floured board and cut into 3-inch circles. Place 1 teaspoon filling in center of one circle, cover with another circle, and seal edges with a fork. Bake at 375°F. for 12 minutes. Makes 2-3 dozen cookies.

❧ DATE FINGERS ❧

An old-fashioned treat appropriate for afternoon tea. Send a small box of good tea along too.

2 eggs
2 tablespoons butter, melted
1 cup sugar
1 cup flour
1 teaspoon baking powder
½ teaspoon salt

1 cup chopped dates
½ cup chopped nuts
¼ cup milk
confectioners' sugar

• • •

box of tea

Beat together eggs, butter, and sugar. Sift together flour, baking powder, and salt; add to egg mixture and blend well. Stir in dates, nuts, and milk. Spread in buttered 8-inch square pan, and bake at 350°F. for 20 minutes. When cool, cut into 1x4-inch fingers, remove from pan, and roll in confectioners' sugar. Makes 16 fingers.

❧ GINGER DROPS ❧

This recipe makes a good hard cookie, an ideal gift for friends with teething babies.

¼ pound butter, softened
½ cup packed brown sugar
3 tablespoons molasses
1 egg

2½ cups flour
½ teaspoon baking soda
2 teaspoons ground ginger
1 teaspoon nutmeg

In mixing bowl, cream butter and sugar; add molasses and egg. Combine dry ingredients, and stir into butter mixture, making a stiff dough. Form into walnut-size balls and press gently onto buttered cookie sheet. Bake at 375°F. for 15 minutes. Makes 4 dozen cookies.

℥ JOE FROGGERS ℥

Man-size molasses cookies — named for an 19th-century sailor, they say. A New England specialty.

¼ cup molasses
4 tablespoons butter, melted
½ cup honey
2 tablespoons hot water
3 tablespoons rum
½ teaspoon baking soda

2 cups whole wheat flour
½ teaspoon ground ginger
¼ teaspoon ground cloves
¼ teaspoon nutmeg
⅛ teaspoon allspice

Combine molasses, butter, honey, hot water, rum, and baking soda. Sift together all other ingredients, and stir in, blending well. Chill dough 1 hour. Use ¼ cup dough for each cookie; make a ball and flatten with the bottom of a glass on buttered cookie sheet, separating cookies by 4 inches. Bake at 375°F. for 10 minutes; cool on rack. Makes ten 4-inch cookies.

℥ LACE COOKIES ℥

An old-fashioned favorite to make — especially for older friends who remember having them as children.

¼ pound butter
¼ cup flour
¾ cup quick-cooking oatmeal

½ cup sugar
2 tablespoons cream

In medium saucepan, melt butter. Combine flour, oatmeal, and sugar; stir into melted butter. Add cream, stirring constantly; remove when mixture begins to bubble. Drop cookie batter by teaspoonfuls 4 inches apart on buttered and floured cookie sheet. Bake 4-5 minutes at 375°F., keeping close watch as these cookies burn very easily. Let cool about 5 minutes before removing with a spatula. Makes about 20 cookies.

❧ *LEMON SLICES* ❧

These taste like lemon pie sandwiches.

PASTRY

½ pound butter, softened
½ cup sifted confectioners' sugar
1 teaspoon lemon juice

½ teaspoon grated lemon rind
2¼ cups sifted flour
¼ teaspoon salt

LEMON FILLING

1 egg, lightly beaten
1 teaspoon grated lemon rind
⅔ cup sugar

3 tablespoons lemon juice
1½ tablespoons butter

In mixing bowl, cream butter and sugar; add lemon juice and lemon rind. Stir in flour and salt. Mix well, and refrigerate for at least 1 hour. Sprinkle marble slab or board with more confectioners' sugar, and roll out dough. Cut into 2½-inch circles, then cut each circle in half. Bake semicircles on ungreased cookie sheets at 400°F. for 4-6 minutes.

To make lemon filling, mix ingredients in double boiler top; cook until thick, stirring constantly. Remove from heat and let cool.

When cookies are cool, frost one semicircle with filling, and top with another semicircle to make a sandwich. Makes about 3 dozen cookies.

❧ *MAGIC COOKIE SQUARES* ❧

A crunchy-sweet coconut-flavored goody.

¼ pound butter, melted
1½ cups graham cracker crumbs
1 cup chopped walnuts or
  pecans
6-ounce package semisweet
  chocolate chips

1⅓ cups (3½-ounce can) flaked
  coconut
13-ounce can sweetened
  condensed milk

Pour melted butter into bottom of 9x13-inch pan. Layer the other ingredients in order, and bake at 350°F. for 25 minutes, or until lightly browned on top. Cool 15 minutes before cutting. Makes 18 squares.

❧ COLORED HOLIDAY
SUGAR COOKIES ❧

Let your imagination run free with these brightly colored cookies. Make your own designs out of cardboard (place cardboard pattern on top of rolled dough and cut around it). You can frost them, too, after baking (see page 93 for frosting).

½ pound butter, softened
1½ cups sugar
3 eggs, lightly beaten
½ cup sour cream
½ teaspoon vanilla

4 cups flour
1 teaspoon salt
liquid or paste food coloring in
   different colors

In large mixing bowl, cream butter and sugar until light and fluffy. Add eggs, sour cream, and vanilla; then gradually add flour mixed with salt. Shape dough into 2 balls, cover with plastic, and refrigerate over-night. Work on half of the dough at a time, keeping other half refrigerated. Break off small portions, and work in desired amounts of food coloring. Roll out dough on floured surface, cut into desired shapes, and highlight with colored dough detail (you don't need to moisten the dough pieces — they'll stick). Bake on buttered cookie sheets at 350°F. for 10-12 minutes. Poke hole in each cookie while still soft, cool on rack, and insert ribbon hanger in hole. Makes about 30 decorated cookies.

❧ PECAN COOKIES ❧

These cookies make an attractive addition to a holiday assortment.

¼ pound butter, softened
½ cup packed brown sugar
1 egg
1 teaspoon vanilla

1 cup flour
1 teaspoon cinnamon
½ teaspoon nutmeg
12 pecans, halved

In mixing bowl, cream butter and sugar; add egg and vanilla. Combine dry ingredients and beat in; drop dough by rounded teaspoonfuls onto buttered cookie sheets. Press a nut half on top of each cookie. Bake at 350°F. for 10-12 minutes. Makes 2 dozen cookies.

✂ LIZ AND BEN'S HOLIDAY SUGAR COOKIES (any holiday will do) ✂

When children make these (and mine have been making them from the age of 6), part of the ritual is eating about one-quarter of the dough raw, eating all broken cookies and holes from wreaths, sampling portions of frosting, and devouring just-frosted cookies that look especially good. About five cookies per batch survive to be given to school friends. If you decide to make these delicious cookies for gifts, best keep the children out of the kitchen.

COOKIES

½ pound plus 1 tablespoon butter, melted	1½ teaspoons vanilla
1½ cups sugar	3¾ cups sifted flour
3 eggs	1½ teaspoons baking powder
	1½ teaspoons salt

In mixing bowl, beat together butter, sugar, eggs, and vanilla. Sift together dry ingredients, and beat into egg/butter mixture. Chill at least 1 hour. Roll out dough, a quarter at a time, on lightly floured board. Cut with floured cookie cutters. Place on ungreased cookie sheet and bake at 400°F. for 6-8 minutes, or until delicately golden. Makes about 4 dozen cookies.

FROSTING

6 tablespoons butter, softened	1 pound confectioners' sugar
1 teaspoon vanilla extract	3-4 tablespoons milk
¼ teaspoon salt	food coloring

In medium bowl, cream butter and vanilla; add salt and confectioners' sugar and mix well. Gradually add milk, being careful not to add too much, or frosting will drip off cookies. Liz and Ben prefer richly colored cookies and therefore, add about half a bottle of food coloring; their favorite shade is kelly green. You can divide the frosting up in separate bowls, and tint each batch a different color.

✼ SCOTTISH SHORTBREAD ✼

Pack the shortbread in a colorful tin box, as the Scots themselves do. Wonderful with French cocoa (page 115).

½ pound butter, softened
½ cup confectioners' sugar
⅛ teaspoon salt

2½ cups pastry flour
confectioners' sugar

In mixing bowl, cream butter and sugar until smooth. Add salt, then gradually stir in flour. Turn out onto floured board and knead 5 minutes. Pat dough into 9-inch square pan, and prick deeply all over with a fork. Bake at 225°F. for 1 hour, or until light brown. Remove from oven and sprinkle with confectioners' sugar. Cut into squares.

✼ MOXIE "COOKIES" ✼

My friend Susan Mahnke makes these biscuits for her dog Moxie — your own canine friends will appreciate them too.

3½ cups whole wheat flour
3 cups rolled oats
½ cup powdered milk
½ cup bacon grease
2 teaspoons cod liver oil
2 eggs
1½ cups instant beef gravy

Combine all ingredients into a sticky dough. Drop by tablespoons onto ungreased cookie sheet and bake at 325°F. for 50 minutes. Cool on rack and store in plastic bag. Makes about 30 dog cookies.

❧ FAVORITE OATMEAL COOKIES ❧

For years this was the only way my children would eat cereal.
These cookies hold up well in the mail.

¼ pound butter, softened
1 cup packed brown sugar
½ cup granulated sugar
2 eggs
¼ cup water
1 teaspoon vanilla

3 cups rolled oats
1 cup flour
1 teaspoon salt
½ teaspoon baking soda
1 teaspoon cinnamon

In mixing bowl, beat together butter, sugars, eggs, water, and vanilla. Add remaining ingredients and mix well. Drop by rounded teaspoonfuls on buttered cookie sheets and bake at 375°F. for 12 minutes. Makes abut 4 dozen cookies.

❧ PEANUT BUTTER
AND JELLY THUMBPRINTS ❧

A sure-fire children's cookie for school occasions.

¼ pound butter, softened
½ cup peanut butter
½ cup packed brown sugar
1 egg
½ teaspoon vanilla

1¼ cups flour
½ teaspoon baking soda
¼ teaspoon salt
grape (or other) jelly

In mixing bowl, cream butter, peanut butter, and sugar; add egg and vanilla. Combine dry ingredients, and stir in; mix well. Form walnut-size balls, and place on buttered cookie sheets. Press thumb into top of each cookie, and fill indentation with jelly. Bake at 350°F. for 6-8 minutes. Makes about 2 dozen cookies.

BARBARA'S COLORED SALT/CLAY DOUGH (inedible)

*T*hough this dough and anything made from it cannot be eaten, it is so versatile and so innovative I can't resist including it. Then too, gifts made from it, being inedible, are more or less lasting. Years ago, my sister-in-law, Barbara Navas, began making Christmas gifts out of baker's clay, a simple flour and salt dough, to present to family and friends. As she gradually refined her techniques, elevating her dough figures to an art form, she began selling them wholesale to gift shops and through craft fairs. Last year, this endeavor became a year-round business. She presently puts in more ten-hour days than she likes to think about in her kitchen, with almost more business than she can handle. Here is her recipe for dough, along with the method she invented for coloring it, and tips she has picked up along the way.

Barbara pre-dyes her dough, which makes colors much more vibrant than dough that is painted later. To color dough, add tempera powder of desired shade into the flour and salt, before adding water.

❧ BARBARA'S BAKER'S CLAY ❧

Recipe may be doubled or tripled.

4 cups flour such as Gold Medal or Pillsbury (do *not* use King Arthur brand, as it makes the dough puff up)
1 cup salt

powdered tempera paint (use the more expensive brands because the pigment is better)
1½ cups water

In large mixing bowl, mix dry ingredients together with a fork. Stir in tempera color to desired tint. Add water, and mix well. Turn out onto floured board and knead for 10 minutes. (If you don't plan to use all the dough at once, cover the unused portion with plastic and refrigerate, but set it out to warm to room temperature before you do use it. Refrigerated dough tends to become more moist. It should therefore be kneaded again when at room temperature, and more flour worked into it if necessary. Dough may be refrigerated for 3-4 days.) If weather is hot or humid, refrigerate dough, working with small portions at a time.

After kneading, roll out dough and cut out cookie ornaments, plaques, Christmas cards, etc.; prick rolled-out dough with a fine needle to allow air to escape. Hair for figures is created by pressing dough through a garlic press or sieve. When appliquéing pieces onto figures, pat with moistened finger to facilitate sticking.

Barbara uses clay sculpture tools for details. One of her most popular items is a decorated mirror frame; she bakes the frame and glues the mirror on later with ceramic glue. (She found that baking the frame with the mirror tends to crack the mirror.) Items that don't melt — glass beads for eyes, non-corrosive* metal buttons, paperclips, hooks, wood — may be baked in the dough. Baker's clay items should be baked on ungreased cookie sheets at 275°F. for 3-7 hours, depending on thickness. Items are done when they pop up from the cookie sheet, and sound hollow when tapped.

The baked clay figures are quite delicate — like bisque. Use a protective coating to harden the dough, to prevent breakage, as well as to protect the figures from moisture. Barbara dips her pieces into transparent polyurethane, and hangs them, or places them on a rack or screen to dry.

Even with the protective coating, baker's clay items should not decorate a bathroom, hang over the stove, or be stored or exhibited in an excessively humid location — the basement for example. With a little care, however, salt clay figures and ornaments may last for generations.

A thoughtful added touch would be a gift tin box in which the ornament could be stored.

Don't use metal that can rust or corrode, as it rots the dough from the inside.

⚔ CHAPTER 5 ⚔
Appetizers, Salads, and Beverages

*T*his selection of foods makes excellent hostess and holiday gifts, though of course they do yeoman duty (especially the salads) as contributions to potluck suppers, and other events requiring food for admission. Some, like Jere Morris's iced tea, are old family standbys, but special enough to make a gift for some lucky friend.

PACKAGING FOR APPETIZERS, SALADS, AND BEVERAGES

Appetizers, salads, and beverages are most appropriate as hostess gifts or as contributions to potluck meals of any kind.

If you don't use your own dishes — to be retrieved later — for appetizers, use foil trays or paper plates covered with plastic wrap. Clear glass or plastic bowls are attractive for salads.

You can be more fancy with beverages, as inexpensive and pretty bottles are easy to find these days at any kitchen specialty shop. Personalized labels are easy to obtain (Miles Kimball, Bond Street, Oshkosh, WI 54901), but if you can, make your own on blank labels from the stationery store. Gift bottles *may* be mailed, though be sure you wrap them in plastic, and package in a cardboard box with plenty of buffer material. Thermos bottles are in order for hot drinks to be used on the spot.

APPETIZERS

Originally appetizers were supposed to whet the appetite, but many of the ones that follow are rich enough to satisfy it.

ANN MORRIS'S CHEESE-BACON HORS D'OEUVRES

A nutty, cheesy, tasty, hot hors d'oeuvre.

½ pound Cheddar cheese, sliced
½ pound cooked bacon
10-ounce package slivered almonds
1 small onion, chopped
1 teaspoon Worcestershire sauce
mayonnaise
party rye bread

Put first five ingredients into a blender and puree. Add enough mayonnaise to bind. Spread on party rye slices. Just before serving, place under broiler until spread is hot and bubbly. Makes about 1 pound of spread — enough to serve a crowd.

✄ CHEESE STRAWS ✄

A homemade cheese stick, from Hope Taylor.

1 pound sharp Cheddar cheese, grated fine
¼ pound butter, softened

2 cups flour
¼ teaspoon cayenne
salt

In mixing bowl, combine cheese and butter. Blend in flour sifted with cayenne. Roll out on floured board and cut in 1½x½-inch rectangles. Sprinkle with salt. Bake on ungreased cookie sheets at 400°F. for 8-10 minutes. Makes about 10 dozen.

✄ SPICY CLAM DIP ✄

An appetizer that can double as a light meal. Serve like fondue. Accompanying instructions should advise reheating in a 300°F. oven. Bread cubes and vegetables should be packaged in separate plastic bags.

two 8-ounce packages cream cheese, softened
three 6½-ounce cans chopped clams, drained (except ¼ cup liquor)
2 tablespoons grated onion
¼ cup dry white wine
2 teaspoons Worcestershire sauce
1 teaspoon Tabasco sauce
1 teaspoon horseradish

½ teaspoon salt
1 tablespoon chopped fresh savory or chopped fresh parsley
• • •
Cut raw vegetables to dip: carrots, celery, broccoli, cauliflower, scallions
French bread (page 00), cut in cubes

In medium heavy saucepan, beat cream cheese until smooth. Beat in other ingredients; cook over low heat for 3-4 minutes, stirring constantly, until mixture bubbles; cool. Pour mixture into heat-resistant 1-quart casserole. Serves 8-12.

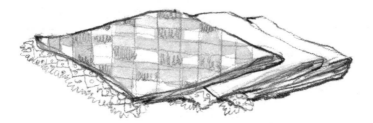

FETA CHEESE ROLLS

Easy to make and always a hit. Reheat under broiler, briefly.

8 ounces cream cheese, softened
8 ounces feta cheese, softened
2-2½ tablespoons cream
two 8-ounce cans crescent dinner rolls
¼ pound butter, melted

In mixing bowl, blend together cheeses and cream; set aside. Open one can of rolls at a time, and cut into eight triangles of dough along perforations. Next cut each triangle in half. Brush each small triangle with melted butter, drop a rounded teaspoonful of cheese mixture in middle, and roll up point first. Brush top of roll with butter; repeat until thirty-two little cheese rolls are made. Place on lightly buttered cookie sheets, and bake at 350°F. for 8 minutes, or until rolls are golden. Makes 32 rolls.

GUACAMOLE

This mellow version of the famous Mexican dip goes well with chili (page 28). Include a bag of tortilla or corn chips.

2 ripe avocados, peeled and chopped
1 ripe tomato, peeled and chopped
1 small onion, chopped
1 clove garlic, pressed
2 tablespoons fresh lemon juice
1 tablespoon (or less) chopped green chilis
1 teaspoon salt
¼ teaspoon cayenne
¼ teaspoon pepper

• • •

bag of tortilla chips or corn chips

If avocados are hard when you buy them, leave them in a closed paper bag on the counter; they'll ripen faster. To peel tomato easily, dip in boiling water. Put all ingredients in blender and puree. Pack in small crocks or 3-inch soufflé dishes, cover with plastic wrap, and chill. Do not leave dip uncovered for long, as avocado tends to darken. Makes 3 cups.

⚡ HANCOCK DIP ⚡

A recipe locally famous in Hancock, New Hampshire, supplied by Dorothee English. Send a box of crackers or a bag of potato chips along with the dip. Instruct to reheat, covered, at 325°F. for 10 minutes.

two 8-ounce packages cream
  cheese
1 cup sour cream
2½ ounces dried beef, chopped
  fine
½ envelope onion soup mix

½ green pepper, chopped fine
1 teaspoon Worcestershire sauce
¾ cup chopped walnuts
• • •
crackers or potato chips

Beat all ingredients — except walnuts and crackers or chips — together in oven-proof 1-quart casserole. Sprinkle walnuts over top and bake, uncovered, in a 325°F. oven for 30 minutes. Should be served warm, with crackers or potato chips. Serves 8-12.

⚡ KIPPER SPREAD ⚡

An unusual and delicious hors d'oeuvre for seafood lovers. Pack as gift in small plastic-wrap-covered crocks. Advise to spread on thin wheat crackers, topped by a slice of pimiento-stuffed olives. (You can include the crackers and olives with the gift.)

3¼-ounce can kippered snacks,
  drained
4 anchovy fillets
4 ounces cream cheese, softened
1 teaspoon Dijon mustard
1 clove garlic

1 tablespoon chopped fresh
  oregano
1 tablespoon fresh lemon juice
sour cream
• • •
wheat crackers
jar stuffed olives

Puree kippered snacks, anchovies, cream cheese, mustard, garlic, oregano, and lemon juice in blender; add enough sour cream to give mixture consistency of smooth paste. Chill in refrigerator. Makes about 1 cup.

❦ LIVER PÂTÉ ❦

Everyone has his favorite; this is mine.

1 onion, chopped
1 clove garlic, pressed
¼ pound butter
1½ pounds chicken livers, cut in
   pieces
¼ cup dry white wine
2 hardboiled eggs, cut in pieces

¾ teaspoon dry mustard
¼ teaspoon sage
¼ teaspoon thyme
½ teaspoon salt
pepper
sour cream

In heavy enamel or stainless-steel frying pan, sauté onion and garlic in 3 tablespoons butter; puree in blender. Sauté chicken livers in remaining butter until brown; stir in wine and cook for 3-4 minutes, stirring constantly. Puree livers, wine, eggs, and seasonings in blender, adding sour cream as needed to form thick, smooth paste. Pack in small ceramic crocks or 3-inch soufflé dishes, and cover with plastic wrap; refrigerate. Pâté should stay in refrigerator no longer than 3 days. Recipe may be frozen if you seal the top with melted butter, and then plastic wrap. Makes 3 cups.

❦ COCKTAIL MEATBALLS ❦

Delicately flavored, and elegant. Serve with toothpicks. Include a box, if you remember. Instructions should advise to reheat, covered, at 350°F. for 10-15 minutes.

¾ pound lean ground beef
¾ pound sausage meat
¼ cup flour
1 cup sour cream
⅓ cup Ritz cracker crumbs
2 scallions, minced
1 tablespoon chopped fresh
   parsley
2 eggs

1 teaspoon grated lemon rind
1 teaspoon salt
½ teaspoon sage
pepper to taste
3 tablespoons vegetable oil
2 tablespoons butter
• • •
box of toothpicks

Mix all ingredients — except oil and butter — together and form into 1-inch balls. Heat oil and butter in large frying pan and brown meatballs uniformly (about 10 minutes). Makes about thirty 1-inch balls.

✄ DARRAGH KARR'S STUFFED MUSHROOMS ✄

Bread-and-cheese-stuffed mushrooms flavored with onion, garlic, and basil. Reheat briefly under broiler.

1 pound mushrooms	½ cup grated Cheddar cheese
2 tablespoons butter	¼ cup grated Parmesan cheese
½ small onion, chopped	¼ teaspoon basil
1 clove garlic, pressed	salt and pepper to taste
½ cup flavored bread crumbs	vegetable oil

Clean mushrooms. Remove stems, chop fine, and place in mixing bowl; set aside. In small skillet, sauté onion and garlic in butter until tender; add to chopped stems. Add other ingredients and enough oil to give mixture the consistency of stuffing. Stuff caps with mixture, and bake on cookie sheet at 350°F. for 25-30 minutes. Serves 4-6.

✄ HEARTY STUFFED MUSHROOMS ✄

These sausage-stuffed, garlicky mushrooms make a fine prelude to Italian dinners. Reheat under broiler, briefly.

1 pound mushrooms	1 teaspoon oregano
1 pound sweet Italian sausage, casings removed	½ teaspoon salt
1 small onion, finely chopped	¼ teaspoon pepper
3 cloves garlic, minced	½ cup fine bread crumbs
2 tablespoons butter	½ cup freshly grated Parmesan cheese
1 teaspoon basil	2 tablespoons sherry
	2 tablespoons butter, melted

Remove stems from mushroom caps. Chop stems fine and set aside. In heavy frying pan, brown sausage meat; stir in onion, garlic, butter, and mushroom stems. Cook until tender. Stir in all other ingredients except melted butter; let cool and stuff caps. Brush melted butter over stuffing, and bake on cookie sheet at 350°F. for 15 minutes. Serves 4-6.

⚔ ROQUEFORT CHEESE BALLS ⚔

Believe it or not, this is marvelous served spread on molasses macaroons.

8 ounces Roquefort cheese
6 ounces Cheddar-cheese spread
12 ounces cream cheese, softened
2 tablespoons minced onion
1 small clove garlic, pressed

1 tablespoon Worcestershire sauce
½ cup chopped fresh parsley
1 tablespoon chopped fresh chives
1 cup finely chopped walnuts

In a mixing bowl, thoroughly combine the cheeses. Add onion, garlic, Worcestershire sauce, 1 tablespoon parsley, and 1 teaspoon chives. Shape into two balls, cover with plastic wrap, and refrigerate over night. Let balls reach room temperature (about 30 minutes), then roll in mixture of remaining parsley, chives, and nuts. Makes 2 cheese balls.

⚔ SPINACH DIP ⚔

A creamy green dip with a hint of nutmeg. Serve with crackers of choice (Swedish flatbread is excellent). Reheat over low heat on stove top, or in 300°F. oven for 10-15 minutes.

10-ounce package frozen chopped spinach
4 tablespoons butter
3 scallions, chopped
1 clove garlic, pressed
1 cup ricotta cheese
½ cup sour cream
½ cup grated Parmesan cheese
1 egg, beaten
½ cup milk
½ teaspoon salt
pepper to taste
½ teaspoon nutmeg

Cook spinach according to directions, drain well, and set aside. In heavy saucepan, sauté onion and garlic in butter; stir in spinach and other ingredients. Cook 5 minutes over medium heat. Serve warm. Makes about 1 quart of dip.

SALADS

Salads make a welcome addition to dinners as hostess gifts. The recipes below are chosen for portability.

✺ ASPARAGUS SALAD ✺

A superb way to capitalize on fresh spring asparagus.

2 pounds fresh asparagus
1 cup sour cream
3 tablespoons fresh lemon juice
½ cup fresh chopped parsley

1 tablespoon chopped chives
¼ teaspoon tarragon
¼ teaspoon salt
pinch pepper

Remove tough ends from asparagus and steam until tender, but still crisp. Drain and immerse asparagus in cold water; drain again. Cut asparagus into 1½-inch pieces, and place in salad bowl. Combine other ingredients, mix well, and pour over asparagus. Toss gently. Serves 4-6.

✺ GREEN BEANS AND BASIL ✺

A tangy cold bean salad that keeps well in the refrigerator.

1½ pounds green beans, cut into
  1½-inch pieces
½ cup vegetable oil
½ cup wine vinegar
¼ cup chopped fresh basil leaves

1 clove garlic, pressed
½ teaspoon salt
pepper to taste
2 scallions, chopped

Steam green beans until tender for 8-10 minutes, place in bowl or crock, and set aside. Whisk or beat together oil, vinegar, and seasonings; pour over beans. Add scallions and toss gently. Cover and refrigerate. Beans gain in flavor if chilled for 24 hours. Serves 8.

☙ CAESAR SALAD ❧

My father's variation of the famous salad — the perfect complement to grilled meat for summer cookouts. Send the croutons along in a plastic bag.

2 heads Romaine lettuce
   (Boston is also good)
¼ teaspoon dry mustard
¼ teaspoon black pepper
½ teaspoon salt
½ cup grated Parmesan cheese
juice of 2 lemons
6 tablespoons vegetable oil

dash Worcestershire sauce
4-5 anchovy fillets, chopped
2 eggs

• • •

croutons (4 slices of white bread,
   diced, and sautéed in butter
   with pressed garlic clove)

Tear lettuce, place in large salad bowl, and sprinkle with mustard combined with pepper, salt, and cheese. Mix lemon juice, oil, Worcestershire sauce, and anchovies; pour over lettuce. Break 2 raw eggs over salad, and mix well. Just before serving, add croutons. Serves 8-10.

☙ AUNT RUTH'S FRUIT SALAD ❧

A treasured family tradition for after-Thanksgiving supper.

14-ounce can pineapple chunks
½ cup pineapple juice from can
¼ cup fresh lemon juice
¼ cup orange juice
1 cup sugar

2 eggs
½ cup heavy cream, whipped
various fruits cut up: apples,
   bananas, oranges, grapefruit,
   peaches, etc.

In double-boiler top, combine pineapple, pineapple juice, lemon juice, orange juice, sugar and eggs; cook over medium heat, stirring frequently, until thick. Remove from heat and cool. Fold in whipped cream. Arrange fresh fruit in a bowl and pour cream mixture over top. Serve warm. Serves 4-6.

❧ MICA'S LAYERED SALAD ❧

A colorful and crunchy vegetable salad, very attractive made in a glass bowl.

1 head iceberg lettuce, torn into bite-size chunks
2 scallions, cut up
2 carrots, sliced
10-ounce package frozen peas, cooked

8 water chestnuts, sliced
1 pint mayonnaise
½ cup grated Parmesan cheese
½ pound bacon, cooked crisp and crumbled

In salad bowl, layer first five ingredients in order given. Spread mayonnaise over top, and sprinkle with cheese and bacon. Cover with plastic wrap and chill. Serves 4-6.

❧ HOT GERMAN POTATO SALAD ❧

This is an old family favorite which makes a nice complement to roast pork or ham.

6 medium potatoes, peeled and boiled
6 slices bacon
1 medium onion, chopped
2 tablespoons flour
1 tablespoon sugar

1½ teaspoons salt
½ teaspoon celery salt
pepper to taste
¾ cup water
⅓ cup vinegar

Slice potatoes and set aside. In heavy frying pan, cook bacon; drain on paper towel. Sauté onion in bacon fat; blend in flour, sugar, salt, celery salt, and pepper. Cook over low heat until smooth and bubbly. Remove from heat, and stir in water and vinegar. Heat to boiling, stirring constantly; boil 1 minute. Gently mix in potatoes and crumbled bacon. Remove from heat. Serves 6-8.

❧ *FRENCH POTATO SALAD* ❧

Potato salad with mustard, wine, and herbs. Serve at room temperature.

20 new potatoes, or 10 average-
  size potatoes
water to cover
½ cup dry white wine
1 tablespoon Dijon mustard
½ cup red wine vinegar
¾ cup vegetable oil

2 tablespoons fresh chopped
  parsley
1½ teaspoons chopped fresh
  thyme
6 scallions, chopped
salt and pepper to taste

In large pot, bring potatoes (skins on for new potatoes; larger potatoes should be peeled and cut into quarters) to boil in water to cover. Cook at low boil for 15 minutes, or until potatoes are cooked through, but still firm. Drain and cool; cut into ½-inch slices, and place in large bowl. Toss lightly with white wine. In another bowl, combine other ingredients; pour over potatoes and toss gently. Cover with plastic wrap until ready to serve. Serves 8.

❦ MUSHROOM SALAD ❦

A really deluxe side dish for any buffet.

2 tablespoons butter
1 tablespoon olive oil
2 anchovy fillets
2 cups sliced mushrooms
1 clove garlic, pressed
2 tablespoons dry white wine
2 tablespoons fresh lemon juice
¼ pound Provolone cheese, cubed
¼ pound Genoa salami, cubed

¼ pound prosciutto ham, cubed
½ cup chopped onion
¼ cup sliced black olives
2 tablespoons chopped fresh parsley
1 tablespoon fresh oregano, or 1 teaspoon dried
½ cup olive oil
½ cup red wine vinegar
salt and pepper to taste

In heavy enamel or stainless steel frying pan, heat butter and 1 tablespoon olive oil; add anchovies and mash into a paste. Add mushrooms and garlic, and sauté over medium heat, stirring until mushrooms are lightly browned. Add wine and 1 tablespoon lemon juice; simmer gently 5 minutes, stirring continually. Remove from heat and place in 1-quart crock. Add cheese, meat, onion, olives, parsley, and oregano. Beat together ½ cup olive oil, red wine vinegar, remaining tablespoon of lemon juice, salt, and pepper, and pour over ingredients in crock. Refrigerate at least 2 hours. Serves 4-6.

❦ TABOULI ❦

This famous near-Eastern concoction makes a wonderful side dish, but is so filling that it can easily pinch-hit as a light supper or a picnic lunch. Tabouli gains in flavor as it ages, and if you don't watch out becomes addictive.

1 cup bulgar wheat
1 cup boiling water
2 tomatoes, diced
1 small onion, chopped
1 green pepper, chopped
1 stalk celery, chopped

4 radishes, diced
½ cup chopped parsley
½ cup chopped mint leaves
½ cup fresh lemon juice
¼ cup vegetable oil
1 teaspoon salt

Pour boiling water over bulgar wheat and let sit 1 hour; drain. Mix in other ingredients; chill 12-24 hours. Serves 4.

⚔ ANN MORRIS'S
STUFFED TOMATOES ⚔

An easy and elegant addition to any meal. Transport in covered baking dish, and reheat for 15 minutes at 300°F.

6 large tomatoes
salt
¾ cup seasoned bread crumbs
½ cup grated Cheddar cheese
½ cup fresh chopped parsley

½ teaspoon garlic salt
pepper to taste
vegetable oil
butter

Cut tomatoes in half. Scoop out pulp and reserve. Sprinkle tomato halves with salt, and turn upside down to drain. Place tomato pulp in mixing bowl with bread crumbs, cheese, parsley, garlic salt, pepper, and enough vegetable oil to bind. Fill tomatoes with mixture and place in greased baking dish. Put a pat of butter on top of each, and bake at 375°F. for 20-30 minutes. Serves 6.

⚔ MARINATED VEGETABLES ⚔

For those with bountiful gardens, this is a wonderful way to share the wealth.

4 cups assorted vegetables: cut-up cauliflower, broccoli, carrots, Brussels sprouts, squash, etc.
¾ cup olive oil
¼ cup fresh lemon juice
2 cloves garlic, pressed

1 teaspoon Dijon mustard
½ teaspoon salt
pepper to taste
1 tablespoon fresh chopped oregano
1 egg, coddled*

Steam vegetables individually, until just tender. Place in large bowl. In small bowl, combine oil, lemon juice, and seasonings; beat with a whisk. Beat in egg. Pour dressing over vegetables, and let marinate at room temperature for a few hours, or refrigerate overnight. Serves 4-6.

To coddle egg, place egg in cold water and bring just to boil. Remove egg. It is now coddled.

BEVERAGES

The drink recipes below are primarily for entertaining — to be brought to parties as hostess gifts, or given for holidays, birthdays, or anniversary occasions, when such a gift would be appropriate and useful. But a few, like Hot Eggnog and Cold Curative, are fine restorative drinks — welcome gifts for ailing friends.

❧ BLACKBERRY CORDIAL ❧

A warming after-dinner drink; also a scrumptious sauce for ice cream. Bottle in glass jar — or bottle with screw-on top. This cordial is a beautiful shade of deep red, and decorative, clear-glass bottles show it to advantage. May be stored at room temperature. Makes 7-8 cups.

8 cups ripe blackberries	pinch cloves
1 cup water	pinch nutmeg
2 cups sugar	2 tablespoons fresh lemon juice
¼ teaspoon cinnamon	3 cups vodka

Place berries in heavy enamel or stainless-steel saucepan, and crush with potato masher. Add water, cover, and heat to boiling over medium heat. Simmer gently for 10 minutes, stirring occasionally.

Line a sieve with three layers of cheesecloth, or with a coffeemaker-size coffee filter, and place sieve over a bowl. Pour in blackberries and juice, lightly pressing blackberries to wring out juice. There should be about 4 cups of juice. Discard pulp. Put juice back in heavy saucepan; add sugar, cinnamon, cloves, and nutmeg. Stir over medium heat until sugar is dissolved; boil gently 3 minutes. Remove from heat and cool. Stir in lemon juice and vodka. Makes 7-8 cups.

⚔ MULLED CIDER ⚔

A hot drink for cool autumn evenings, or to bring to a Bonfire Party. Bring cinnamon sticks along in a bag, and place one in each steaming cup.

1 quart cider
¼ cup orange juice
2 tablespoons fresh lemon juice
1 tablespoon brown sugar
1½ teaspoons cinnamon

¼ teaspoon ground cloves
½ teaspoon nutmeg
• • •
4 cinnamon sticks

Combine ingredients in saucepan and heat to boiling. Pour into 1-quart thermos. Makes 1 quart.

⚔ HOT CLAMMY MARY ⚔

A fine restorative to bring along to football games or any other cold weather activities. You can store this in a covered container in the refrigerator; accompanying instructions should state that it may be served hot or cold, despite its name.

20-ounce can of Clamato juice
2 beef bouillon cubes
5 drops Tabasco sauce

1 tablespoon fresh lemon juice
3 scallions, chopped
1½ cups vodka

In heavy enamel or stainless-steel saucepan, combine all ingredients except vodka; boil gently 2 minutes, or until bouillon cubes are dissolved. Remove from heat; cool 5 minutes. Add vodka. Pour into 1-quart thermos to transport. Makes 1 quart.

❧ FRENCH COCOA ❧

A fabulous cold-weather treat for all ages. Note that the cocoa should not be allowed to boil when being reheated.

¾ cup semisweet chocolate bits
½ cup light corn syrup
½ cup sugar
⅓ cup water

1 teaspoon vanilla
2 cups whipping cream
1 quart milk

In heavy saucepan, combine chocolate bits, corn syrup, sugar, and water; cook over low heat until blended. Remove from heat and stir in vanilla. In a separate saucepan, scald milk and cream together (do not boil). Stir in chocolate/sugar mixture. When uniformly blended, remove from heat and fill thermoses. Makes 2 quarts.

❧ HOPE TAYLOR'S COFFEE LIQUEUR ❧

A homemade liqueur, less expensive than the commercial brands, but every bit as good. This will keep up to a month on the shelf — longer in the refrigerator.

2 cups water
1½ cups granulated sugar
1½ cups packed light brown
  sugar

⅓ cup instant coffee
1 fifth vodka
2 teaspoons vanilla

In heavy saucepan, combine water and sugars, and simmer, uncovered, for 10 minutes. Remove from heat, stir in instant coffee, and cool. Add vodka and vanilla; mix well. Pour into bottles and cork or cap. Makes about 6 cups.

❧ SANDY TAYLOR'S COLD CURATIVE ❧

This may not actually cure a cold, but it certainly makes the patient feel better! Double the recipe and pour into a pint-sized thermos for a sick friend.

2 ounces whiskey
1 tablespoon honey
3 tablespoons frozen orange juice concentrate, preferably thawed

4-5 ounces hot (not boiling) water
lemon juice to taste
1 lemon wedge

Stir all ingredients together in a mug. Squeeze juice from lemon wedge into drink. Makes 1 cup.

❧ CRANBERRY CORDIAL ❧

Perfect for a Thanksgiving hostess gift. For a non-alcoholic beverage, substitute gingerale or soda water for the vodka.

1 quart cranberries
1½ cups water
pinch salt

1 cup sugar
¼ cup lemon juice
vodka

In enamel or stainless-steel saucepan, cook cranberries with water for 10 minutes, or until skins pop. Strain juice through cheesecloth-lined sieve into bowl. Discard pulp. Return juice to saucepan; add salt, sugar, and lemon juice; bring to boil. Remove from heat, measure, and add vodka to the amount of half the juice measure. Makes about 4 cups.

❧ FROTHY HOT EGGNOG ❧

This drink is a treat for sick kids who need never know that it's nutritious. For sick adults, substitute a tablespoon of rum for the vanilla. Not for tummy bugs, however.

4 eggs, separated
½ cup sugar
½ teaspoon cinnamon
¼ teaspoon salt

3 cups milk
1 teaspoon vanilla
1 tablespoon sugar
nutmeg

In heavy saucepan, blend egg yolks, ½ cup sugar, cinnamon, and salt. Beat in milk until thoroughly blended. Cook over medium heat until bubbles form at edge (do not boil). Remove from heat and add vanilla. In separate bowl, beat egg whites until frothy. Gradually beat in 1 tablespoon sugar until it forms soft peaks. Fill 4 mugs with meringue, pour egg yolk mixture over, and sprinkle nutmeg on top. Makes 4 mugs.

⚶ *LIMONADA* ⚶

This Basque "lemonade" makes a delicious and refreshing summer drink. Accompanying instructions should suggest to serve cold in chilled wine glasses.

6 lemons
1 cup sugar
1 bottle dry red wine (750 ml.)

1 bottle dry white wine (750 ml.) — I use a Soave

Carefully peel the yellow zest from 3 lemons and cut zest into strips. Cut remaining 3 lemons crosswise, into rounds. In 3-quart container, squeeze juice from the 3 peeled lemons; stir in sugar and both wines. Add lemon peel and rounds. Refrigerate for several hours. Serves 8.

⚶ *RASPBERRY SHRUB* ⚶

A traditional summer drink, as pretty as it is delicious. A few whole raspberries and lemon slices should accompany the bottle of shrub in plastic sandwich bags.

1 quart raspberries
2 cups water
1 cup sugar
¼ cup fresh lemon juice

1 lemon
• • •
lemon slices
whole raspberries

Place raspberries in heavy, enamel or stainless-steel saucepan, and crush gently. Add water and sugar, cover, and boil gently for 10 minutes. Strain out pulp through cheesecloth-lined sieve; discard pulp. Add lemon juice and chill. Serve in chilled tumblers. Store in refrigerator. Serves 4.

✂ SANGRÍA ✂

This Spanish drink tastes much better made from scratch than the store-bought variety. Include a bottle of club soda, to be mixed in according to personal taste when the sangría is served.

1 bottle dry red wine (750 ml.)
¼ cup brandy
½ lemon, sliced
½ apple, cored and cut into
   wedges

½ orange, sliced
¼-½ cup sugar
  • • •
club soda

Combine all ingredients, except club soda, in a large covered container; chill for several hours before giving. Serves 6-8.

✂ JERE MORRIS'S ICED TEA ✂

Jere's mother, Dot Morris, used to keep a pitcher of this tea on hand in the refrigerator all summer long. Mint and lemon may be strained out before pouring into gift container; but fresh mint sprigs should be included in a plastic bag as garnish.

8 tea bags
(1½ cups sugar)
1 lemon, sliced
handful fresh mint
1 quart boiling water

two 4-ounce cans frozen orange
   juice concentrate
3 cups cold water
  • • •
fresh mint sprigs

In 2-quart pitcher, place tea bags, optional sugar, lemon, and mint. Add boiling water, and let steep for 1 hour. Remove tea bags, then add orange juice concentrate and cold water. Chill in refrigerator at least 2 hours. Makes 2 quarts.

⚜ *CHAPTER 6* ⚜

Jellies and Preserves, Pickles and Relishes, Condiments and Special Seasonings

*P*reserves of all kinds are probably the oldest types of kitchen gifts, simply because they are small, easily transported, and will keep indefinitely. With the age of refrigeration, preserving has become something of a lost art and like breadmaking, has acquired a mystique. But once you get down to it, preserving isn't difficult at all, especially if you use screw-top jars. In fact, a jar of good home-made preserves is a real treat, especially to city dwellers. The condiments and special seasonings given here also keep very well, and make excellent year-round gifts.

PACKAGING JELLIES AND PRESERVES, PICKLES AND RELISHES, CONDIMENTS AND SPECIAL SEASONINGS

The simplest and most straightforward containers for jellies and preserves are, of course, canning jars. The screw-top variety are the easiest to use, but the old wire-bail Atlas and Ball (etc.) jars can still be found cheaply at yard sales and flea markets. The ones made of pale blue glass especially have nostalgic charm. And you can still obtain the rubbers for sealing at the sort of hardware stores that keep their screws in bins.

For jams and jellies sealed with paraffin, you have more flexibility. Jams and jellies do not generally require processing. Choose any fancy glasses you want, as long as the gauge is up to sterilization. Pretty bottles and jars are readily available in kitchen specialty shops, or to make a gift very special, use antique glassware.

All of the gifts in this chapter* may be mailed (use sturdy corrugated boxes and plenty of packing material). If you wish to mail a number of jams, jellies, or pickles to a single address, your liquor store can give you corrugated box dividers from their cases of bottles. Cut them down to fit your containers.

*Except Big Sur Salad Dressing, and Whitney's Artichoke Dip.

JELLIES AND PRESERVES

A note on proper procedure for pouring and sealing jams and jellies, as excerpted from *The Forgotten Art of Making Old-Fashioned Jellies, Jams, Preserves, Conserves, Marmalades, Butters, Honeys, and Leathers,* published by Yankee, Inc., Dublin, New Hampshire, 1977.

• • •

Wash and sterilize your glasses (and caps if you use them) by heating in a kettle of cold water that is gradually brought to the boiling point. Turn off the heat and leave the glasses in the kettle until ready to use. (Jars should still be hot when you pour in the jelly.) When the preserves are ready, drain the glasses and set out on a level surface. Skim the foam off the jelly or preserves, taking care not to stir it in. Ladle the jelly or preserves into the glasses, holding ladle close to the glass as you pour, to help eliminate air bubbles, and being careful not to allow any jelly or preserves to dribble onto the rim at the top of the glass. Leave ⅛ inch headroom with modern screw-band tops or ½ inch headroom when using paraffin to seal the jars. If you do slop, wipe jar rim clean before sealing. When the jars are filled, insert a teaspoon in the middle of each jar and stir the jelly around once to eliminate air bubbles. Then seal.

If you use screw-band tops without paraffin, put on the cap and screw band tightly. Invert the glass for a second, then turn right side up. The jar will form a vacuum seal as the jam or jelly cools.

If you use paraffin, have it ready and melted. It is safer to melt paraffin like baking chocolate — in a double boiler — but if you watch it carefully (**you can end up with a stove fire),** you can melt it over direct heat. You want it just melted, not smoky.

Pour a thin layer of melted paraffin over the jam or jelly, taking the glass in your hand and tilting it slightly, so that the paraffin flows to every part of the rim, to ensure a perfect seal. Prick any air bubbles that appear in the wax. As the wax cools, these bubbles will turn into holes in the paraffin layer, and therefore the seal. When the wax is cool and firm, cover each glass with a metal top — or a circle of paper or foil secured with a rubber band or masking tape. Label each glass and store in a cool, dark place. One final note — do not double the recipes that follow — the recipe will either not jell or not be as good. Instead, make two or more separate batches.

❧ HOPE TAYLOR'S GRAPE OR BLACKBERRY JELLY ❧

Especially good if made from wild grapes. For blackberry jelly, substitute 2 quarts blackberries for the grapes, then follow the same procedure.

3½ pounds blue grapes, with seeds
5 cups water

5 cups sugar
1¾-ounce box fruit pectin

Place grapes or blackberries in large kettle and crush gently with masher. Add water and bring to boil; cover pot, reduce heat, and simmer 15 minutes. Strain grapes or berries through cheesecloth jelly bag. Discard pulp. Measure juice. You should have about 5 cups. Return juice to pot, add sugar and pectin, and boil for 1 minute. Skim and fill hot sterilized jars. Seal. Makes five ½-pint jars.

❧ HOPE TAYLOR'S CRAB APPLE JELLY ❧

Apple jelly is good, but crab apple jelly is better. Use 6-ounce jars — this is too rare a treat to make up in ½-pint jars.

5 pounds crab apples, quartered
5 cups water

1¾-ounce box fruit pectin
6½ cups sugar

Place apples and water in heavy saucepan and bring to boil. Turn down heat, cover pan, and simmer apples for 15 minutes. Crush apples in saucepan, then pour into cheesecloth jelly bag, and let drip through (will take a while). When dripped through, you should have about 7 cups of juice. Discard pulp. Put juice in saucepan and add pectin. Bring to boil, then add sugar. Boil 1 minute, skim off foam, and pour into hot, sterilized jars. Makes eight 6-ounce jars.

⚜ HOPE TAYLOR'S MINT JELLY ⚜

Give this gloriously green mint jelly with a matching glass of purple grape jelly for a color-coordinated Christmas gift — or by itself any time. Mint jelly is good with many meats, but is traditionally served with lamb.

6 pounds apples, cored, peeled, and quartered
6 cups water
3 cups sugar

12 large sprigs fresh mint
2 tablespoons lemon juice
1¾-ounce box fruit pectin
2 drops green food coloring

Place apples and water in large pot. Bring to boil. Reduce heat, cover, and simmer 20 minutes. Strain apples and water through a jelly bag (or four layers of cheesecloth); reserve juice. Discard pulp. Put juice, sugar, mint, lemon juice, pectin, and food coloring into pot, bring to boil, and boil for 5 minutes, stirring frequently. Remove from heat. Skim top, strain, and pour into hot, sterilized jars and seal. Makes four ½-pint jars.

⚜ MADEIRA JELLY ⚜

An exquisite, spiced-wine jelly for high teas. To be served with white bread slices spread with cream cheese.

4 cloves
½ teaspoon cinnamon
pinch nutmeg
½ cup dried apricots
1 cup water

2 cups Madeira wine
½ cup fresh lemon juice
1¾-ounce box fruit pectin
3 cups sugar

Place cloves, cinnamon, nutmeg, apricots, and water in enamel or stainless-steel pot; bring to boil, reduce heat, cover, and simmer 20 minutes. Add Madeira, lemon juice, pectin, and sugar; bring to boil and boil 2 minutes. Strain, pour into hot, sterilized jars, and seal. Makes five ½-pint jars.

✠ HOT PEPPER JELLY ✠

Serve this tangy green jelly with meat, or on crackers spread with cream cheese.

2 green peppers, chopped and seeded
2 hot green chili peppers, chopped and seeded

1½ cups cider vinegar
5½ cups sugar
1¾-ounce box fruit pectin
(2-3 drops green food coloring)

Purée peppers with vinegar in a blender, then place puree in saucepan. Bring to boil, and add sugar. Stirring constantly, bring back to boil, and boil 1 minute. Skim foam from top, then add pectin and optional food coloring. Cool and spoon into hot, sterilized jars. Seal. Makes four ½-pint jars.

✠ BEN'S BANANA JAM ✠

An old-fashioned spread for sandwiches and breakfast toast. Store in refrigerator.

6 bananas, peeled
1¼ cups apple juice
4 tablespoons fresh lemon juice

¼ teaspoon cinnamon
pinch cloves

Place all ingredients in enamel or stainless-steel pot, bring to boil, and boil gently until smooth and bubbly. Turn down heat, and simmer 5 minutes more, stirring frequently. Spoon into hot, sterilized jars. Makes five ½-pint jars.

✠ FOUR-FRUIT JAM ✠

A rich red jam with a blend of fruit flavors.

2 cups sliced peaches
1 quart whole strawberries, hulled
1 quart red cherries, pitted

1 quart raspberries
½ cup fresh lemon juice
water
8 cups sugar

Place fruit in large pot, add just enough water to be seen, and stir in sugar. Bring to boil, stirring constantly. Reduce heat, and simmer about 30 minutes until jam begins to thicken, stirring often to prevent sticking. Pour into hot sterilized jars and seal. Makes ten ½-pint jars.

✺ HOPE TAYLOR'S STRAWBERRY JAM ✺

Better than the kind you buy because there's a higher percentage of fruit.

2 quarts strawberries, hulled and crushed
5 cups water

1¾-ounce box fruit pectin
5 cups sugar

Put strawberries, water, and pectin into heavy saucepan, and bring to full boil. Stir in sugar at once. Stirring constantly, bring back to full boil. Still stirring, boil 1 minute. Remove from heat, and skim off foam. Pour jam into hot, sterilized jars, and seal. Makes ten ½-pint jars.

✺ ORANGE-CRANBERRY COMPOTE ✺

An attractive Christmas dessert which can be kept, refrigerated, for months. Serve warm (not hot) in a dish by itself, or over ice cream. May be served chilled, or at room temperature. The compote should be stored in the refrigerator until used, for aesthetic reasons (the fruit will not spoil, but it will become murky in appearance if stored at room temperature).

1½ cups fresh cranberries
1½ cups water
1½ cups dry white wine
¾ cup sugar
1 teaspoon grated orange rind

½ teaspoon cinnamon
pinch nutmeg
4 oranges, peeled and segmented
¼ cup orange liqueur

In heavy enamel or stainless-steel saucepan, combine cranberries, water, wine, sugar, grated rind, cinnamon, and nutmeg. Heat to boiling; reduce heat, cover, and simmer 5 minutes. Add orange segments, cover, and simmer 4 minutes more. Remove from heat, and stir in orange liqueur. Spoon compote into two glass pint jars with screw tops (do not pressure seal). Makes 2 pints.

✣ CITRUS MARMALADE ✣

A mild grapefruity marmalade.

zest of 1 grapefruit	4 cups water
zest of 2 oranges	4 cups sugar
zest of 1 lemon	1¾-ounce box fruit pectin

Squeeze juice from grapefruit, oranges, and lemon; reserve in refrigerator for other use. Slice zests in julienne slivers, and place with water in pot, cover, and let stand overnight. After 24 hours, bring to boil, turn down heat, cover, and simmer for 2 hours, or until zest is tender. Let stand another 24 hours. Add sugar and pectin, bring to a boil, and cook 2 minutes. Skim and pour into hot, sterilized jars. Seal. Makes four ½-pint jars.

✣ LEMON MARMALADE ✣

This delicate, all-lemon marmalade takes some fussing as it does not use pectin. For the gourmets on your gift list, who will appreciate the fussing.

3 unpeeled lemons, thinly sliced	2½ cups sugar
5 cups water	(4 drops yellow food coloring)

Cut lemon slices in half, catching any juice in bowl. Place slices, juice, and water in enamel or stainless-steel pot. Heat to boiling; reduce heat and simmer 30 minutes, uncovered. Measure liquid and add water as necessary to bring up to 3 cups. Return to pot and add sugar and food coloring if desired. Cook over medium high heat 30-35 minutes, stirring frequently. Marmalade should be firm enough to set when it coats a spoon. Pour into hot sterilized jars, and seal. Makes three ½-pint jars.

✖ STRAWBERRY-ORANGE MARMALADE ✖

The perfect gift for friends who love both strawberry jam and orange marmalade — it's like both.

2 oranges
2 lemons
½ cup water
⅛ teaspoon baking soda
1 quart strawberries, hulled and crushed

6 cups sugar
half a 6-ounce bottle liquid pectin

Peel oranges and lemons, discard white portion, and chop zests fine. In heavy saucepan, place zests, water, and soda; bring to boil. Turn down heat, cover, and simmer 20 minutes. Add thinly sliced oranges and lemons; cover, and simmer 20 minutes more. Add crushed strawberries and sugar; bring to boil. Boil 5 minutes, stirring frequently. Remove from heat, stir in fruit pectin, let stand 5 minutes, then skim. Pour into hot sterilized jars, and seal. Makes eight ½-pint jars.

✖ RHUBARB-ORANGE PRESERVES ✖

This spicy rhubarb jam provides a breath of spring all year round.

8 cups chopped rhubarb
8 cups sugar
2 tablespoons grated orange rind
1 teaspoon allspice

½ teaspoon cardamom
½ cup fresh lemon juice
1 cup orange juice
6-ounce bottle liquid pectin

In large enamel or stainless-steel pot, combine rhubarb and sugar; cover pot tightly, and let sit overnight. Add next five ingredients, and bring to a boil; reduce heat, and simmer for about 10 minutes. Remove from heat, and add pectin. Pour into hot, sterilized jars, and seal. Makes 5 pints.

⚜ APRICOT-PECAN CONSERVE ⚜

Use with or without butter as a spread with turkey, pork, or ham, to make great sandwiches; or with cream cheese to make tea sandwiches.

1 pound dried apricots, chopped
water to cover
1½ cups orange juice
grated rind of 1 orange

grated rind and juice of 1 lemon
3½ cups sugar
¾ cup chopped pecans

In enamel or stainless-steel saucepan, simmer apricots in water to cover for 30 minutes. Drain apricots, discard water, and add to apricots orange juice, orange and lemon rinds, lemon juice, and sugar. Cook over medium heat 2 hours, stirring constantly. Stir in nuts, and pour into hot, sterilized jars. Makes five ½-pint jars.

⚜ PEACH CONSERVE ⚜

Peach jam gingered up with orange and lemon.

1 orange, thinly sliced
7 cups fresh peach chunks
5 cups sugar

½ cup fresh lemon juice
½ teaspoon ground ginger

Cut orange slices in half. In heavy enamel or stainless-steel saucepan, combine all ingredients. Bring to boil, reduce heat, cover, and simmer 1 hour, stirring frequently. Pour into hot, sterilized jars, and seal. Makes seven ½-pint jars.

PICKLES AND RELISHES

Wash and sterilize canning jars according to the directions at the beginning of the chapter (page 121). For processing, place the filled and covered sterilized jars in a boiling water bath (jars to be placed on a rack, with enough space between them to let water circulate, and deep enough so an inch of water will cover the tops.) When water returns to a boil, begin counting processing time. Individual times are given for each recipe where processing is required. (Excerpted from: The Forgotten Art of Making Old-Fashioned Pickles, Relishes, Chutneys, Sauces and Catsups, Mincemeats, Beverages and Syrups, *Yankee, Inc., Dublin, New Hampshire, 1978.)*

✕ BREAD AND BUTTER PICKLES ✕

This method makes extra-crispy pickles.

8 cups unpared, thinly sliced
   cucumbers
6 onions, peeled and sliced thin
3 cloves garlic, pressed
⅓ cup kosher salt
10 cups cracked ice

5 cups sugar
3 cups cider vinegar
2 tablespoons mustard seed
1½ tablespoons celery seed
1½ teaspoons turmeric

In large enamel or stainless-steel pot, combine cucumbers, onions, and garlic. Add salt, cover with cracked ice, and mix thoroughly. Let stand 3 hours; drain well. Combine with remaining ingredients, and heat just to boiling. Remove from heat immediately, and fill hot sterilized jars. Seal and process 10 minutes. Makes 7 to 8 pints.

✺ *PICKLED CRAB APPLES* ✺

A pretty and tasty garnish for roast pork or poultry — and salads.

2 quarts sound, whole crab
  apples, with stems
1½ tablespoons whole cloves
2 cinnamon sticks, crumbled

pinch nutmeg
6 cups packed brown sugar
3 cups cider vinegar
3 cups water

Pierce crab apples with large needle to keep them from bursting. In large enamel or stainless-steel pot, place cloves and cinnamon sticks enclosed in a tea ball or cheesecloth bag. Add nutmeg, sugar, vinegar, and water. Bring to boil, and boil 5 minutes. Add apples, and simmer until tender. Cover and let stand 24 hours in a cool place. Stir with wooden spoon once or twice gently, while standing. Return to stove, bring to boil, boil 1 minute, and spoon into hot sterilized jars. Cap and process 10 minutes. Makes 6 pints.

✺ *MUSTARD PICKLES* ✺

Pickled garden vegetables in an eye-appealing combination.

20 medium cucumbers
1 quart small onions
2 heads cauliflower
2 quarts green tomatoes
3 green peppers, chopped
3 red peppers, chopped
1 cup kosher salt

8 cups sugar
½ cup dry mustard
1 cup flour
1 tablespoon turmeric
1 quart vinegar
1 quart water

Cut cucumbers, onions, cauliflower, and tomatoes into bite-size pieces. Place each vegetable (including chopped peppers) in separate containers, divide up salt among them, and let stand overnight. Mix dry ingredients in large enamel or stainless-steel pot, add vinegar and water, and heat to boiling. Add vegetables, and simmer until mixture is thick and vegetables are tender. Pour into hot, sterilized jars, seal, and process for 10 minutes. Makes 8 pints.

✖ BLUEBERRY RELISH ✖

An off-beat blueberry-flavored relish to serve with cold meats, or with crackers spread with cream cheese.

3 cups sugar
1½ cups water
3 pints blueberries
1½ cups cider vinegar
1 teaspoon grated lemon rind

2 teaspoons cinnamon
1 teaspoon allspice
¼ teaspoon cloves
1¾-ounce box fruit pectin

In heavy enamel or stainless-steel saucepan, combine sugar and water; boil 1 minute. Add blueberries and return to boil; reduce heat, cover, and simmer 5 minutes. Add remaining ingredients, bring back to boil, and boil 2 minutes more. Pour into hot sterilized jars. Seal and process 10 minutes. Makes 3 pints.

✖ OLD-FASHIONED CRANBERRY RELISH ✖

A traditional holiday gift, to serve with Thanksgiving turkey or Christmas goose — but good any time of year. This relish will keep two to three weeks in the refrigerator, or can be frozen.

4 cups fresh cranberries
4 oranges, peeled, seeded, and
  sectioned
4 unpeeled apples, cored and
  quartered

3 lemons, peeled, seeded, and
  sectioned
4 cups sugar

Put cranberries, oranges, apples, and lemons through a food grinder, or use blender or food processor on coarse grind. Combine ground fruit with sugar. Mix well. Pour into screw-top jars. Screw tops tight and store in refrigerator. Makes 3 quarts.

❧ *PEPPER RELISH* ❧

Making pepper relish used to be an annual fall project among the Navas and Chace families in Riverside, Rhode Island. It is still a fun family project, and produces so much relish that you have to give at least half of it away.

12 red peppers, chopped
12 green peppers, chopped
12 medium onions, chopped

1 quart cider vinegar
2½ cups sugar

Place all ingredients together in enamel or stainless-steel pot. Bring to boil, then simmer 15 minutes uncovered. Pour into hot, sterilized jars. Seal and process 10 minutes. Makes about 9 pints.

❧ *UNCOOKED TOMATO RELISH* ❧

A delicious shortcut relish for hot dogs that needs no processing, but will keep all winter in the refrigerator.

¼ bushel firm red tomatoes,
chopped (about 12 cups)
½ cup kosher salt
2 cups diced fresh celery
2 green peppers, seeded and
chopped

1 large onion, chopped
2 cups sugar
4 cups cider vinegar
4 tablespoons mustard seed
½ cup salt

Sprinkle chopped tomatoes with kosher salt and let stand overnight. Drain thoroughly. Add all other ingredients, ladle into jars, and cap. Must be refrigerated. Makes 7-8 pints.

✄ HOPE TAYLOR'S ZUCCHINI RELISH ✄

One solution to the gardener's perennial zucchini problem; or a fine revenge on those who gave you their excess zucchinis.

6 medium zucchinis, unpeeled, sliced fine	2 cups packed brown sugar
	½ teaspoon turmeric
5 medium onions, thinly sliced	¼ teaspoon ground cloves
5 peppers, seeded and chopped fine	1 tablespoon mustard seed
	½ teaspoon celery seed
¼ cup kosher salt	2 cups cider vinegar

In large enamel or stainless-steel pot, combine vegetables and salt; let stand 3 hours. Rinse and drain, then set aside. Combine remaining ingredients in pot, bring to boil, and boil 1 minute. Add vegetables to hot syrup, stir well, and simmer 5 minutes more. Spoon mixture into hot, sterilized jars. Seal and process 10 minutes. Makes 8 pints.

CONDIMENTS AND SPECIAL SEASONINGS

☆ BARBECUE SAUCE ☆

This is much tastier than the store-bought variety, and a good substitute for catsup as well.

24 large, firm red tomatoes, peeled, cored, and chopped
4 medium onions, chopped
2 cups chopped celery
3 green or red peppers, chopped
2 hot red peppers, chopped
1½ cups water
1 cup packed brown sugar

½ cup vinegar
½ cup fresh lemon juice
2 cloves garlic, pressed
1 tablespoon salt
½ teaspoon pepper
1 tablespoon paprika
2-3 drops Tabasco sauce
4 cups vegetable oil

In enamel or stainless-steel pot, place tomatoes, onions, celery, peppers, and water; bring to boil, cover, and simmer 30 minutes, or until vegetables are soft. Puree in blender, then return to pot and add other ingredients. Cover and simmer slowly 2 hours, stirring frequently, until mixture has the consistency of catsup; pour into hot sterilized jars, and seal. Process 10 minutes. Makes 7 pints.

✥ MAJOR STONE'S CHUTNEY ✥

A recipe we developed after my husband returned from a trip to Pakistan. Due to a printing error in the Indian cookbook we were using (twelve cups of vinegar were called for rather than two), the steam from the first batch we made killed all of the tomato seedlings on my kitchen windowsill. Made as below, this apricot/apple chutney goes well with curries, or with roast pork or turkey.

1 pound dried apricots, chopped	2 cups cider vinegar
3 tart apples, peeled, cored, and quartered	2 teaspoons salt
	½ teaspoon dry mustard
1 large onion, chopped	1 teaspoon ground ginger
1 cup seedless raisins	½ teaspoon ground cloves
3 cups packed brown sugar	⅛ teaspoon cayenne

In heavy enamel or stainless-steel saucepan, combine all ingredients and bring to boil. Turn down heat, cover, and simmer gently 2 hours, or until thick and darkened. Stir frequently. Spoon into hot, sterilized jars, seal, and process 10 minutes. Makes five ½-pint jars.

✥ RHUBARB CHUTNEY ✥

Include a jar of this chutney with Curried Chicken (page 28) or Cassoulet (page 25) for a truly lavish gift — or the chutney alone, with recipes for these dishes.

4 cups rhubarb, cut into 1-inch pieces	1 cup cider vinegar
	½ cup raisins
2 cups packed brown sugar	1 teaspoon ground ginger
1 large onion, chopped	½ teaspoon cinnamon

Combine all ingredients in large enamel or stainless-steel saucepan. Bring to boil; reduce heat to medium, cover, and simmer 1 hour, or until mixture thickens. Stir frequently. Spoon into hot, sterilized jars and seal. Process 10 minutes. Makes four ½-pint jars.

❧ *BOUQUETS GARNIS* ❧

Simple, inexpensive, and thoughtful gifts. Enclose these flavor-giving herb/spice mixtures in tea balls, or in cheesecloth bags tied with colorful rick-rack or ribbon. In the bouquets garnis *given below, combine all ingredients in tea ball or cheesecloth bag and place in soup or casserole while cooking. Remove* bouquets garnis *before serving.*

LEMON HERB *GARNI (use in soups, chicken dishes, seafood, or vegetables)*

1 teaspoon dried lemon peel (sold commercially)

6 cloves

½ teaspoon rosemary

1 bay leaf

SPICE BALL *(for mulled wine and cider)*

1 cinnamon stick, broken into pieces

4 whole cloves

1 whole allspice

½ teaspoon grated nutmeg

1 teaspoon dried orange peel (sold commercially)

CHICKEN-TURKEY SOUP BALL *(send along with a gift of Zesty Turkey Soup, page 22)*

1 bay leaf

12 peppercorns

8 cloves

¼ teaspoon thyme

❊❊❊❊❊❊❊❊❊❊❊❊❊❊❊❊❊❊❊❊❊❊❊❊❊❊❊❊

*T*he two recipes given below may be made in any quantity, depending on the measurement you wish to assign to the term "part." For example, should you assign ¼ cup as "one part," the Big Sur Dressing would require 1¼ cups oil, ½ cup vinegar, ½ cup Dijon mustard, and ¼ cup lemon juice. With salt and pepper to taste, you would end up with 2½ cups Big Sur Dressing.

Similarly, taking the same ¼-cup measurement as "one part," Whitney's Artichoke Dip would require ¾ cup mayonnaise and ¼ cup vinegar, to make 1 cup of Artichoke Dip.

❊ BIG SUR SALAD DRESSING ❊

This dressing is wonderful with avocado salads, and a good all-purpose dressing as well.

5 parts oil	1 part fresh lemon juice
2 parts vinegar	salt and pepper
2 parts Dijon mustard	

Mix all ingredients in a blender; bottle, and refrigerate.

❊ WHITNEY'S ARTICHOKE DIP ❊

To serve with steamed artichokes. Tastes better than melted butter, and is practically labor-free. Give with several large and perfect artichokes. Put your name on the hand-written label, and no one need know that you owe your soul to Cain's or Hellmann's.

3 parts mayonnaise   1 part vinegar

Mix ingredients thoroughly, and spoon into an impressive-looking jar. Keep refrigerated.

✕ HERB BUTTERS ✕

Give all four as a simple but original gift, for those who have everything. To be used for rolls, meat fondues, or vegetables. Instructions should advise to have butters at room temperature before serving. These butters gain in flavor if refrigerated for 1-2 days before being used. Make sure you label each crock of butter with the flavor used. "Tarragon Butter," "Parsley Butter," et al.

1 pound unsalted butter,
  softened
2 teaspoons chopped chives
2 garlic cloves, pressed

2 teaspoons chopped tarragon
1 tablespoon chopped fresh
  parsley

Work butter with a masher in a bowl, or with a spatula on a marble slab; divide into four portions. Work one seasoning separately into each portion. Fill ½-cup crocks and seal with plastic wrap. Makes four ½-cup crocks.

✕ FANCY HERB VINEGAR ✕

Give this in a pretty bottle, with a porcelain stopper if you can find one — two gifts in one. Very nice for salads.

1½ cups white vinegar
2 cloves garlic
½ cup chopped parsley
1 cup chopped tarragon
½ cup dry white wine

Combine all ingredients in a jar with a tight-fitting lid. Discard garlic after 2 days. After 2 weeks, strain and bottle. Store in refrigerator. Makes 2 cups.

✻ *RECIPE INDEX* ✻

⚜ RECIPE INDEX ⚜

Cookies, Bars, and Baker's Clay

Jellies and Preserves

Pickles and Relishes

Pies (see also Tarts)

✠ *ABOUT THE AUTHOR* ✠

Deborah Navas is a writer and editor who (though she grew up in Rhode Island) lives in Peterborough, New Hampshire, with her children and cats. She has had short fiction, poetry, nonfiction, and photography published in a number of magazines. She works as fiction editor for *Yankee* magazine, and as copy editor for *Popular Computing.* With her children she canoes, cross-country skis, climbs Mt. Monadnock annually, and cooks.

KITCHEN GIFT RECORD

Recipe	Given to	Occasion	Date	Comments